# PROCESS SYSTEM VALUE AND EXERGOECONOMIC PERFORMANCE OF CAPTIVE POWER PLANTS

DR. SHOURI P V

SUMESH K T

PARTRIDGE

**To order additional copies of this book, contact**
Partridge India
000 800 919 0634 (Call Free)
+91 000 80091 90634 (Outside India)
orders.india@partridgepublishing.com

www.partridgepublishing.com/india

# CONTENTS

# LIST OF FIGURES

# LIST OF TABLES

# ABSTRACT

*Keywords: Availability, Captive Power Plant, First Law Efficiency, Reliability, Second Law Efficiency, Exergy, Economics*

The economic performance of power plants have received significant notice in today's modern world. An important parameter that remain as the key performance indicator of power plants of modern times is the plant availability. The out-dated layouts, components and fuel systems designed of olden times built during plant establishment periods are subject to modifications in terms of configurations, plant size, retrofit, renovations and fuel systems with the objective of enhanced economic performance and improved plant availability. In today's world of depleting energy resources, the importance for energy conservation policies and frame works are high and the outlook towards economic performance of plants and their reliability and availability after process system modifications is highly specific.

This book presents the impact of the modifications done in De-Super heater and Flame Burner System of a Boiler during conversion from Oil fired to LNG fired system on the process system value of 7MW Captive power plant of a fertilizer process industry. The project also examines the criticality of LNG price variation on the modified processes. First Law Efficiency analysis and Second law efficiency analysis are also done on major components of the captive power plant and results are analyzed before and after modifications.

# CHAPTER 1

# INTRODUCTION

## 1.0 Introduction

This section figures out basic concepts upon which the thesis is developed around a captive power plant system. The introductory chapter concludes with a summary of the organization of the thesis including identification of the general content of specific chapters and appendices. The basic concepts on which the book is developed are Reliability, Availability, Efficiency based on First Law of thermodynamics and Efficiency based on Second Law of Thermodynamics.

## 1.1 Reliability

Reliability is defined as the probability of a system performing its purpose adequately for a period of time intended under the operating conditions encountered. [Etienne Human,2012]

The definition can be break down into four basic parts, namely:

➤ Probability
➤ Adequate Performance
➤ Time
➤ Operating conditions

Probability is the numerical input for the assessments to be conducted. Adequate performance is its "best" performance. There is always a time linked to it, for example a week or a month [Etienne Human, 2012]. The last thing is the operating conditions that are part of the performance of the system or equipment.

Reliability Engineering is the following, in order of priority:

➢ To apply engineering knowledge and with it specialized techniques to present or reduce the likelihood or frequency of failures.
➢ The identification and correction of the causes of failures that do occur, despite the efforts to prevent them.
➢ To determine ways of coping with failures, if their causes have not been corrected for some season or it is not possible to correct it.
➢ Apply method of estimating the likely reliability of new designs, and also for analysing reliability data.

The above four points describe Reliability Engineering.

To the user of a product, reliability is measured by a long, failure free, operation. Long periods of failure free interruptions results in increased productive capability while requiring fewer spare parts and less manpower for maintenance activities which results in lower costs. To the supplier of a product, reliability is measured by completing a failure free warranty period under specified operating conditions with few failures during the design life of the product. Improving reliability occurs at an increased capital cost but brings with it the expectation for improving availability, decreasing downtime and smaller maintenance costs, improved secondary failure costs, and results in better chances for making money because the equipment is free from failures for longer periods of time. While general calculations of reliability pertain to constant failure rates, detailed calculations of reliability are based on consideration of the failure mode which may be infant mortality (decreasing failure rates with time), chance failure (constant failure rates with time), or wear-out (increasing failure rates with time). A few key words describing reliability in quantitative words are: mean time to failure, mean time between failures, mean time between/before maintenance actions, mean time between/before repairs, mean life of units in counting units such as hours or cycles, failure rates, and the maximum number of failures in a specified time interval.

In the context of power generation facilities reliability data are applied at different phases. Reliability data should be applied during construction, production and maintenance of power plants [Dr. P.V. Shouri, Dr. P.S.Sreejith, 2008]. The data may be used for:

- planning of the production park
- benchmarking
- trend analysis
- improving plant components
- risk related to overhauls
- Reliability Centred Maintenance (RCM)
- High Impact Low Probability (HILP) failures
- spare parts optimisation
- Design review
- Optimum redundancy
- Structural reliability
- RAM specification

Asked to name the most important trait of a power plant—reliability, availability, or maintainability—most facility owners and operators would say reliability. But is it really?

It is true that a power plant is a system of interdependent subsystems and that, if one of the subsystems fails, the entire power plant may be at risk of shutting down—a case for reliability being the most important trait. It also is true that most of the components in a power plant have parts that are rotating, reciprocating, or experiencing some type of stress cycle (thermal or mechanical), often under harsh conditions, and if the components are not monitored and maintained properly, they can fail quickly—a case for maintainability being the most important trait. However, it also is true that, most of the time, equipment must be shut down for maintenance to be performed. [Brian Wodka,2013] If a boiler is shut down for cleaning and inspection, it cannot generate steam. It may be extremely reliable, but it is unavailable the week it is shut down. With a power plant providing a utility typically required continuously, availability—the probability of functionality when required—is the most important trait of a power plant. Plant availability is a critical driver for the economic performance of a plant [H. Paul Barringer,1997].

How can availability be maximized? [H. Paul Barringer,1997].A function of both reliability and maintainability, availability can be improved by maximizing uptime (reliability supplemented or enhanced by redundancy) and minimizing downtime (high maintainability).

Maximize uptime, minimize downtime—not unexpected advice. Still, it is much easier said than done.

## 1.2 Maintainability

Maintainability is defined as the probability of performing a successful repair action within a given time. In other words, maintainability measures the ease and speed with which a system can be restored to operational status after a failure occurs. This is similar to system reliability analysis except that the random variable of interest in maintainability analysis is time-to-repair rather than time-to-failure. For example, if it is said that a particular component has a 90% maintainability for one hour, this means that there is a 90% probability that the component will be repaired within an hour. When we combine system maintainability analysis with system reliability analysis, we can obtain many useful results concerning the overall performance (availability, uptime, downtime, etc.) that will help to make decisions about the design and/or operation of a repairable system. [http://www.reliasoft.in/BlockSim/maintainability_analysis.htm,2014]

### 1.2.1 Types of Maintenance

*Reactive.* Commonly referred to as "run to failure" (see "Running (Literally) to Failure," *HPAC Engineering*, September 2010, *http://bit.ly/ Arnold_0910*), reactive maintenance involves ignoring equipment until it fails. It is appropriate for inexpensive, non-critical pieces of equipment (e.g., light bulbs). The problem with it is that failures usually cannot be anticipated. Also, repair costs are higher because of the premium that must be paid for immediate response.

**Preventive.** Recommended in most equipment operation-and-maintenance manuals, preventive maintenance occurs on a schedule. Its basis is the concept that the likelihood of failure is proportional to the age or operating hours of equipment. The idea is that maintenance is better performed too often than not often enough. Changing the oil in a car falls into this category.

This form of maintenance has intrinsic cost ramifications that can be significant. More importantly, it has been shown to be ineffective in controlling failure rates, the reason being the probability of failure does not necessarily increase with age, and maintenance performed in excess increases the opportunity for human error and can shorten the life of parts. [http://www.reliasoft.in/BlockSim/maintainability_analysis.htm]

**Predictive/condition-based.** During the 1980s, the concept of predictive, or condition-based, maintenance came about. The underlying concept of predictive maintenance is, "If it ain't broke, don't fix it." Equipment is inspected routinely, with maintenance performed only as needed. The determining factor is a chosen indicator, such as a squealing belt on belt-driven equipment. Inspections are performed while equipment is operating so as not to affect availability. The idea is to maximize operation and avoid unnecessary maintenance. The problem with predictive maintenance is that it is only as good as the indicator(s) chosen to determine whether maintenance is needed and the interval at which inspections are performed. [http://www.reliasoft.in/BlockSim/maintainability_analysis.htm]

**Reliability-centered.** With predictive maintenance, power-plant operators with limited resources found they were wasting much time frequently checking insignificant items. This led to the development of reliability-centered maintenance, whereby maintenance tasks are prioritized according to risk using analytical methods, such as fault trees, or failure-modes-and-effects analysis.[http://www.reliasoft.in/ BlockSim/maintainability_analysis.htm]

## 1.3 Availability

Availability [H. Paul Barringer,1997] can be defined as the probability that an item will be available when required, or as the proportion of total time the item will be available for use. The proportion of total time that the item is available is the steady state availability. Availability deals with the duration of up-time for operations and is a measure of *how often* the system is alive and well. It is often expressed as (up-time)/(up-time + downtime) with many different variants. Up-time and downtime refer to dichotomized conditions. Up-time refers to a capability to perform the task and downtime refers to not being able to perform the task, i.e., uptime and not downtime. Also availability may be the product of many different terms such as:

$$A = A_{hardware} * A_{software} * A_{humans} * A_{interfaces} * A_{process}$$

and similar configurations. Availability issues deal with at least three main factors (Davidson1988) for: 1) increasing time to failure, 2) decreasing downtime due to repairs or scheduledmaintenance, and 3) accomplishing items 1 and 2 in a cost effective manner. As availability grows, the capacity for making money increases because the equipment is inservice a larger percent of time.Three frequently used availability terms (Ireson 1996) are explained below.

***Inherent availability*,**[[H. Paul Barringer,1997]] *as seen by maintenance personnel*, (excludes preventive maintenance outages, supply delays, and administrative delays) is defined as:

$$A_i = MTBF/(MTBF + MTTR)$$

***Achieved availability*** [H. Paul Barringer,1997], *as seen by the maintenance department*, (includes both corrective and preventive maintenance but does not include supply delays and administrative delays) is defined as:

$$A_a = MTBM / (MTBM + MAMT)$$

Where MTBM is mean time between corrective and preventive maintenance actions and MAMT is the mean active maintenance time.

**Operational availability** *as seen by the user*, is defined as:

$$A_o = MTBM/(MTBM + MDT)$$

Where MDT is mean down time.

A few key words describing [H. Paul Barringer,1997] availability in quantitative words are: on-line time, stream factor time, lack of downtime, and a host of local operating terms including a minimum value for operational availability. Even though equipment many not be in actual operation, the production departments wants it available at least a specified amount of time to complete their tasks and thus the need for a minimum availability value. An example of 98% availability for a continuous process says to expect up-time of 0.98*8760 = 8584.8 hr/yr and downtime of 0.02*8760 = 175.2 hrs/yr as availability + unavailability = 1. Now, using the data set provided, the dichotomized availability is 98.6% based on up time = 8205.3 hours and downtime = 112.5 hours. Of course the dichotomized view of availability is simplistic and provides worst case availability numbers. Not all equipment in a train provides binary results of only up or only down—sometimes it's partially up or partially down. Clearly the issue is correctly defining failure. In the practical world, complexities exist in the definitions for when only some of the equipment is available in a train, and the net availability is less than the ideal availability—i.e., a cutback in output occurs because of equipment failure which decreases the idealized output from say 95% to a lower value such as say 87% when failures are correctly defined

A key measure is defining the cutback (and thus loss of availability from a dichotomized viewpoint) when the cutback declines to a level causing financial losses—this is the economic standard for failure. In short, the area under an availability curve can be summed to calculate a practical level of availability and generate higher values for availability than when only dichotomized values are used. Lack of availability is a problem related to primarily to failures of equipment. But the root cause of the failure may lie in different areas than initially expected. Often deterioration, leading to economic failure, causes conflicts in the definitions of reliability, maintainability, and capability—real life issues are rarely simple and independent.

For production purposes, a system must be fully available (ready for service) and reliability (absence of failures) to produce effective results.

## 1.4 Captive Power Plant

Electric power generation is a state controlled subject. Of late, however, government has liberalized captive power generation for the user industry for bridging the demand-supply gap. The fact that public/private industries use captive power answers the question of financial viability. For, the benefit in terms of prevention of marginal loss of production outweighs the cost of captive diesel power generation. Industries which have a high value added for electricity input will naturally insulate themselves through standby power. From the national point of view, the issues are somewhat different. Here the objective of the policy maker will be efficient resource allocation. The alternatives differ for short and long runs. In the short and medium run, power cut is given and the alternatives may be to

- ➢ impose a uniform power cut on industries
- ➢ impose an 'optimal' power cut, minimizing
- ➢ production loss and unemployment
- ➢ allow for captive power generation.

In the long run, power cut is not a constraint, since extra capacity or reserve margin can be provided for. Growing demand and persistent funds constraint are not sufficient arguments to necessitate the continuance of power cuts, since utilities can segment the market and equilibrate the demand and supply by increasing tariffs. Thus, the long run alternatives are whether to satisfy a certain level of peak demand by additional grid capacity or by captive power. [V Ranganathan, Damodar Mall, 1987] The alternatives have to be compared at the margin and therefore it is not the average cost of electricity at the high tension (HT) terminal or the HT tariff that is relevant, but the marginal (average incremental) cost of electricity. This has to be compared with the cost of captive generation at the given level of demand for captive electricity. In cost-benefit terms, the benefit of captive power generation is not the saving in loss of production but the saving by not producing grid electricity since this is the next best alternative. Unit based captive power generation means pressure on costlier and scarcer fossil fuels, loss of economies of scale, and a built-in capacity underutilization. However, it involves much reduced lumpiness in investment and affords quick capacity addition.

The discussion of the historic slump in spot market electricity prices, triggered by an unprecedented fall in demand and the inadequate availability of domestic coal, has forced captive power producers to turn to exchanges for firing their end-use plants, something unseen in the Indian energy sector. [V Ranganathan, Damodar Mall,1987] About a dozen companies, mostly in the cement, fertiliser, textile and paper sectors, are using the low spot-power prices to their advantage by shifting the energy mix of their manufacturing units. Experts say the rise in the number of captive power companies buying power from exchanges is triggered by stalled gas-based captive plants and lack of linkage coal. Owing to the price drop, companies are finding it economically viable to buy from the exchange. The rising participation from captive power companies has further boosted volumes, leading to higher competition and robust price discovery.

Captive power has played an increasingly significant role in Indian industry, both as a back-up source of generation and as the primary power supply for many industrial facilities. Figure 3 shows how each of the different types of [V Ranganathan, Damodar Mall,1987] CPP have grown since 1985. CPPs have grown at a steady and increasing rate since the pre-reform period of the mid 1980s. From 1995 to 2004, captive generation capacity has increased by 68 percent. This upswing indicates the speed of industrial conversion to own generation when faced with high industrial tariffs, poor service and non-availability of grid power. The choice of fuel for a captive plant is highly dependent on the size of the plant, its intended use and fuel availability/price. For back-up generation, smaller, liquid-based internal combustion engines are normally used. For large scale operations with access to coal allocations or gaspipelines, these have been the fuel of choice.

Scripting history in the industrial sector, a major public sector fertiliser company has fully changed over to LNG from Naphtha/Furnace Oil in its ammonia plant and captive power plant boiler facilities. The plants of the cash-strapped company has been undergoing conversion for the past few months in view of availability of LNG through a terminal. The company has so far made an investment of INR 34 crores and INR 13 crores and respectively in converting its ammonia plant and captive power plant boiler facilities to switch over from the traditionally-used naphtha and furnace oil to Re-gassified Liquid Natural Gas (RLNG). The captive power plants were using Though the company has started using LNG in the plants since beginning of September,2013 full fledged operation began on October 5 of the same year. All the boilers in captive power plant have changed over to LNG fuel on September 3,2013. The change over of fuel feed stock of Ammonia plant began on September 21 when ammonia plant was running at 80 percent.The feed stock change over of ammonia plant was done online on September 26 at 80 percent plant load.With LNG being used in its plants, the company has achieved the distinction of the only company using all three solid, liquid and gaseous feedstock for production of ammonia, a major raw material for all fertilizers. Firewood was used in 1940s. Then it switched over to naphtha, now to LNG.

Most significant difference between Naphtha and Natural Gas-based Ammonia plants are in desulphurisation section. Since gas does not contain much sulphur unlike in Naphtha, pre-desulphurisation section need not be operated. Other important aspect is in the hydrogen to carbon ratio, which is high in case of gas. As a result, less steam is consumed in the reforming section and less carbon is generated.

*Fig 1: Captive Power Plant*

The conversion of the plant from one fuel to another one was an engineering challenge. The online changeover of fuel and feedstock in a running ammonia plant was a new engineering feat never attempted before. The scenario of company discussed above has changed in due course of time due to huge variation in the price of LNG. The impact is discussed in detail in later sections. The theme of the book was identified based on the LNG conversion of the captive power plant of the company.

## 1.5 Process System Modifications

The process system modifications are engineering challenges and their impact on Power Plant System reliability is worth investigative.

Typical approaches to achieve high system reliability are: (1) increasing the reliability of system components and (2) using redundant components in various subsystems in the system. The modification of an existing system with a view to improve energy efficiency should consider these factors. The change in system configuration resulting from system modification can adversely affect the system reliability. Any new proposal for improving the energy efficiency of the process or equipments should prove itself to be economically feasible for gaining acceptance for implementation. In order to determine the economic feasibility of the new proposal, the general trend is to compare the benefits that can be derived over the lifetime as well as the operating and maintenance costs with the investment to be made. The change in system configuration [8] resulting from system modification can adversely affect the system reliability. Whenever a process system is to be modified for energy savings, it is important to know the expected change in system value and impact of modifications on Process System Value. [Dr.Shouri P.V, Dr.P.S.Sreejith -2008].

## 1.6 First Law Energy Analysis

The First Law Energy analysis intend to analyse the process system components separately and to identify and quantify the sites having largest energy losses. Energy conservation study is many times focused on energy efficiency. The first law of thermodynamics is used to analyse the energy utilization. First law analysis doesn't use the quality aspect of energy. [Egware H.O and Obanor A,].Energy analysis is the traditional method of assessing the way energy is used in an operation involving the physical or chemical processing of materials and the transfer and/or conversion of energy. This usually entails performing energy balances, which are based on the First Law of Thermodynamics.

Energy analysis [Egware H.O and Obanor A.] of heat and power cycles are today the most common way of evaluating thermal systems regarding, for instance, fuel utilization and electrical efficiency. Throughout the whole 20th century, energy analysis matured and is today considered a well-established tool to evaluate thermal systems.

Energy analysis is founded [Egware H.O and Obanor A.] on the first law of thermodynamics, and together with the continuity equation over the system and its components, this type of analysis becomes a powerful method. The major aim of an energy analysis is to optimize the thermal efficiency of a system.

First Law analysis might suggest that the amount of energy is conserved during a given process, it fails to identify the decline in the quality of the energy, or the reduced availability of the substance to do work, in its final state. It is therefore useful to perform an exergy analysis for the same process to determine the location, cause and magnitude of losses, so that opportunities to improve resource utilization in the process are identified.

Energy analysis helps designers to find ways to improve the performance of a system in a many way. Most of the conventional energy losses optimization method are iterative in nature and require the interpretation of the designer at each iteration. Typical steady state plant operation conditions were determined based on available trending data and the resulting condition of the operation hours. The energy losses from individual components in the plant is calculated based on these operating conditions to determine the true system losses. In this, first law of thermodynamics analysis was performed to evaluate efficiencies and various energy losses.[Raviprakash kurkiya and Sharad chaudhary,2012]

The First Law deals with the amounts of energy of various forms transferred between the system and its surroundings and with the changes in the energy stored in the system. It treats work and heat interactions as equivalent forms of energy in transit and offers no indication about the possibility of a spontaneous process proceeding in a certain direction. The first law places no restriction on the direction of a process, but satisfying the first law does not ensure that the process can actually occur. This inadequacy of the first law to identify whether a process can take place is remedied by introducing another general principle, the second law of thermodynamics. [Vundela Siva Reddy et.al.]

## 1.7 Second Law Efficiency Analysis

Exergy [A. Rashad, and A. El Maihy] is a measure of the maximum capacity of a system to perform useful work as it proceeds to a specified final state in equilibrium with its surroundings. Exergy is generally not conserved as energy but destructed in the system. Exergy destruction is the measure of irreversibility that is the source of performance loss. Therefore, an exergy analysis assessing the magnitude of exergy destruction identifies the location, the magnitude and the source of thermodynamic inefficiencies in a thermal system.

The exergy [Amirabedin Ehsana, M. Zeki Yilmazoglu,2011] of a system is defined as the maximum available work that can be done by the system-environment combination. Higher values of exergy means a higher value of obtainable work. The exergy analysis is the composite of the first and second laws of thermodynamics. In this analysis heat does not have the same value as work, and exergy loss represents a real loss of work. When analysing novel and complex thermal systems, experience needs to be supplemented by more rigorous quantitative analytical tools. Exergy analysis provides those tools and it helps in locating weak spots in a process. This analysis provides a quantitative measure of the quality of the energy in terms of its ability to perform work and leads to a more rational use of energy

For a control volume at steady state the exergy equation can be written as follows,
Exergy = Exergy out in product + Exergy loss + Exergy destruction

The exergetic efficiency is a measure of performance in terms of optimal performance permitted by both first and second law of thermodynamics and is devoid of the drawbacks inherent in the definition of first law efficiency. For a device whose output is either work or heat transfer, it is detained as ratio of energy transfer achieved by device or system to the maximum possible heat or work usefully transferable by any device or system to the maximum possible heat or work usefully transferable by any device or system using the same energy input as the given system. While numerator is same for both first and second law efficiencies, the denominator in latter case brings both laws of thermodynamics directly into the definition of efficiency. First law focuses attention on reading losses, to improve efficiency. The second law efficiency point out that both losses and internal irreversibility need to be examined to improve performance.

The main features of the exergy analysis are:

- The use of mass conservation, the First Law of Thermodynamics and the application of the Second Law of Thermodynamics;
- The analysis aims to maximize the efficient use of energy resources and environmental issues;
- Identify sites of irreversibility and list the losses in order of importance;
- It is an attribute set of the system and the ambient used as a reference.

Analysis of power generation systems is necessary for the efficient use of energy resources [M. Ghazikhani, M. Ahmadzadehtalatapeh,2010]. The first law of thermodynamics is the most common method for energy analysis of systems, but the combined utilization of the first and second law of thermodynamics or exergy analysis provides the tool distinction between energy losses and irreversibilities in the process. By using exergy analysis, any process and component in the system that having the largest exergy destruction can be identified and this in turn helps the designers to improve the system performance. The exergy concept in power generating plants was interested by a number of researchers. For instance, Habib et al. conducted a research on the thermodynamic performance analysis of the Ghazlan power plant in Saudi Arabia. The system was studied based on the first and second law of thermodynamics according to the available data. A full exergy analysis was carried out to identify the component that has the largest exergy destruction in the whole system. The irreversibility of different components was compared as a function of load. They revealed that major exergy destruction or irreversibility occurs in the boiler. They also revealed that first law results were misleading and evaluation should be based on the second law of thermodynamic results.

The first law of thermodynamics (Energy analysis) deals with the quantity of energy and asserts that energy cannot be created or destroyed. The law merely serves as a necessary tool for the bookkeeping of energy during a process and offers no challenges to the engineer. The second law (Exergy analysis), however, deals with the quality of energy. It is concerned with the degradation of energy during a process, the entropy generation, and the lost opportunities to do work; and it offers plenty of room for improvement. The second law of thermodynamics has proved to be a powerful tool in the optimization of complex thermodynamic systems (Ganapathy *et al.*, 2009; Makinde, 2008; Cengel and Boles, 2008).

## 1.8 Motivation

The recent modifications done during the process of fully changeover of the fuel feed stock from Furnace Oil to RLNG of the captive power plant of a fertilizer industry and the opportunity to assess the impact of the modification on the process system value of the plant through the process system evaluation model incorporating reliability and availability was noticed. The industry was a major giant but it is cash strapped over a few years due to various reasons and the feedstock changeover is a major step in the revival process to gain momentum in the economic performance of the plant. During the surveillance visit it is observed that an assessment of the power plant by performing its energy and exergetic analysis and evaluation of efficiencies of major power plant components have not been done by the organization in the context of modifications before and after modifications. The conducted literature survey theoretically supports and signify the practical importance of power plant reliability and availability and the need for incorporating the two parameters in pay back calculations in process system modifications. A significant process system evaluation model is developed and have been recognized through various publications in international energy journals through the works of Dr. Shouri P.V. and Dr. P.S.Sreejith(2008). On account of mentioned factors, the impact assessment of the cash strapped public sector fertilizer industry for its recent modifications in the captive power plant and its energy and exergy analysis and expected results and feedback to industry are believed by the masters research scholar to be worth recognizable contributions to the industry and society and a major breakthrough to interconnect between academics and industry. A process system evaluation model widely acknowledged and discussed among international energy scholars and academic society will be used in the project.

**Structure of Book**

This book is categorized into six chapters. Starting with first chapter titled "Introduction", the book proceed to chapter two titled "Literature Survey". Chapter three describes "Problem formulation" and chapter four details the "Work done and Results". Chapter Five gives a short description on Future work. The conclusion is given in Chapter Six.

# CHAPTER 2

# LITERATURE SURVEY

## 2.1 Reliability Analysis

Reliability analysis is an innate aspect of power plant design and plays considerable role throughout the plant operation in terms of expenses (operating and maintenance) and optimal maintenance scheduling of its equipments. Reliability may be defined as the ability of an equipment, component, product, system, etc., to function under designated operating state of affairs for a specified period of time or number of cycles. In the context of CHP systems, reliability is the probability of generating electricity under operational conditions for a definite period of time. Reliability of a CHP system is a function of maintenance (scheduled or forced) cost, which in turns depends upon the Mean Time Between Failures (MTBF) and Mean Time To Repair (MTTR) of equipment or systems, and which are further dependent on complexity in design, state, age of the equipment or system and to some extent on the availability of spare parts.

Recurring failures that lead to complete power plant outage need repair and proactive maintenance to invigorate power plant performance and reduction monetary losses. Downtime losses and maintenance cost of a CHP system can be reduced by adopting a proper mix of maintenance and repair strategies. In the worst situation, unavailability of an equipment or system affects whole plant and plant trips in this case. But in general, the failure of an equipment or system may not affect the complete plant and therefore its criticality is at some intermediate value. In that case reliability of system comes down and its effect on reliability of other systems is also observed. The criticality level decides the importance of the equipment or system and choice of appropriate maintenance and repair strategy so that reliability may be maintained up to a mark.

In the literature both qualitative and quantitative methods for assessing the reliability of complex systems are available. The most commonly used qualitative methods are Fault Tree Analysis (FTA), Failure Modes, Effects and Criticality Analysis (FMECA), Failure Modes and Effects Analysis (FMEA), Root Cause Analysis (RCA), Root Cause Failure Analysis (RCFA), Fish Bone Analysis (FBA), Event Tree Analysis (ETA), and Predictive Failure Analysis (PFA). Block diagram analysis, Markov chain, and Monte Carlo simulation are some of the quantitative methods of reliability analysis available in the literature.

Various attempts have been made by researchers in developing procedures for the evaluation of the reliability of various systems [M. Mohan *et. al.*,2008], [M. Mohan et. al.,2003], [M. Mohan et. al.,2006], [R.K. Garg et.al.,2006], [M. Mohan et. al.,2004], [K.B. Goode et.al.2000], [D. Bradt,1997] and [O.P.Gandhi,1991]. The two-state Markov model is the mainly used outage model in power system reliability analysis [S. Carlier,1996].

Eti et al. integrated reliability and risk analysis for maintenance policies of a thermal power plant. Need to integrate RAMS (reliability, availability, maintainability and supportability) centered maintenance along with risk analysis was stressed, although results expected or obtained with the application of those concepts were not explained.

A staircase function was introduced by Ji et al. to approximate the aging failure rate in power systems and a component renewal process outage model based on a time-varying failure rate was proposed. The model reflected the effects of component aging and repair activities on the aging failure rate.

Markov method was used by Haghifam and Manbachi to model reliability, availability and mean-time-to-failure indices of combined heat and power (CHP) systems based on interactions between electricity generation, fuel-distribution and heat-generation subsystems. The proposed model can be useful in feasibility studies of CHP systems and in determining their optimal design, placement and operational parameters.

Carpaneto et al. carried out Monte Carlo simulation for identifying long, medium and short-term time frames by incorporating uncertainty at large-scale and small-scale for cogeneration system. Availability coefficient assumed to be independent of year, scenario and control strategy was defined for unavailability of the CHP units, due to scheduled maintenance and reliability aspects, taking into account. Large-scale uncertainty referred to the evolution of energy prices and loads and relevant to the long-term time frame was addressed within multi-year scenario analysis. Small-scale uncertainty relevant to both short-term and medium-term time frames was addressed through probabilistic models and Monte Carlo simulations.

Mohan et al. calculated RTRI (real-time reliability index) for a SPP (steam power plant) using graph theory. Integration of systems and subsystems and interaction among them were considered for the reliability analysis and the proposed methodology can be applied for obtaining availability and maintainability; including optimum selection, bench marking, and sensitivity analysis of SPP. Tang proposed a new method based on the combination of graph theory and Boolean function for assessing reliability of mechanical systems. Graph theory was used for modelling system level reliability and Boolean analysis for interactions. The combination of graph theory and Boolean function bring into being an effective way to evaluate the reliability of a large, complex mechanical system. Garg et al. developed a graph theoretical model to compare various technical and economical features of wind, hydro and thermal power plants.

Performance analysis of coal based steam power plant boiler was carried out by Mohan et al. using graph theory and step-by-step methodology for the evaluation was also proposed. Further graph theory was applied to calculate real-time efficiency index (RTEI) defined as the ratio of the values of variable permanent system structure function

(VPF) in real-time (RT) situation to its achievable design value and in this connection graph theory was used to recommend the an appropriate maintenance strategy for power plants.

The reliability and availability of a CHP depend on the perfect operation of all its systems (e.g., Boiler, Steam turbine and Cooling system). So far researchers evaluated power plant system reliability only at system level without making an allowance for the interactions of systems, and subsystems. Therefore, there is a need for extending the compass of reliability analysis for power plants by taking care of interaction among different systems and subsystems.

A number of approaches and methodologies developed by researchers are available in the literature to model the various systems and their elements. Graph theory is one of such methodologies. It synthesizes the inter-relationship among different parameters and systems to evaluate score for the entire system. Because of its inherent simplicity, graph theory and matrix method have wide range of applications in engineering, science and in numerous other areas [N. Dev et.al.,2013]. Several examples of its use have appeared in the literature [M. Mohan et. al.,2008], [Mohan et. al.,2003], [Mohan et. al.,2006], [R.K.Garg et. al. 2006], [S. Kulkarni,2005], [N.Dev, et.al.,2006], [N.Deo,2007] and [T. Raj, R. Attri,2010] to model the various systems.

The scope of power plant reliability analysis [Brian Wodka,2013] covers:

➢ equipment availability;
➢ plant maintainability;
➢ fuel and water availability; and
➢ power plant reliability in relation to natural hazards.

Though it may seem new and cutting edge [Brian Wodka,2013], reliability-centered maintenance has been around since the 1970s. It started as a government-funded initiative to improve military-aircraft and space missions. By the 1980s, it had proved successful enough that its scope was expanded to the Navy and nuclear industry. During the late 1990s, it was standardized by the Society of Automotive Engineers.[1,2]

In 2000, NASA published the first edition of "Reliability-Centered Maintenance Guide for Facilities and Collateral Equipment."[3]

Despite a proven track record, reliability-centered maintenance [Brian Wodka,2013] has failed to gain widespread acceptance in the industry, largely because of assumptions it is too complex and requires too much work. Where it easily can fail is where most great ideas fail: in the implementation. Experts estimate that as little as 5 percent of reliability-centered maintenance programs are implemented properly. Without the means for proper implementation, even the best-developed reliability-centered maintenance program can be just another (expensive) document sitting on a desk getting ignored.

## 2.2 Achieving Real Results

Reliability availability, maintainability (RAM) is a concept with a history very similar to that of reliability-centred maintenance: Its origins are in the 1970s, and its intent was to assure availability for the military [Brian Wodka,2013]. Whereas reliability-centred maintenance was embraced more for aerospace, RAM primarily was the Department of Defense's protocol for new and advanced combat equipment and weaponry. RAM concentrates more on the design and construction phases than reliability- centred maintenance. For that reason, it tends to be more of an all-encompassing, cradle-to-grave concept.

In 2009, ASME created a committee tasked with reviewing decades of research and documentation related to RAM and developing a standard for new and existing power plants.

The standard, the first draft of which is expected this year, focuses on three key priorities identified by power-plant owners: safety, production, and efficiency. Equipment has been assessed and a judgment as to risk or criticality made. To ensure availability, an appropriate level of reliability and/or redundancy is prescribed and the most appropriate maintenance program (reactive, preventive, predictive/condition-based, reliability-centered) given. Maintenance-program costs are estimated to aid budgeting. The standard can be customized to various facility sizes, risk levels, and budgets.

The standard, requires assignment of a RAM manager, an individual who is responsible for the program's teaching, implementation, and maintenance. A RAM program is a living document permitting continuous improvement and adaptation throughout a power plant's life. This helps to prevent confusion, obsolescence, and, ultimately, disregard. [Brian Wodka,2013]

| | RM | PM | PdM/CBM | RCM | RAM |
|---|---|---|---|---|---|
| Prevents failures | | * | * | * | * |
| Minimizes excess maintenance | * | | * | * | * |
| Prioritizes risk | | | * | * | * |
| Accountability requirements | | | | * | * |
| Reliability specifications | | | | | * |
| Budgetary estimate | | | | | * |

*Fig 2.1: Comparison of RM/PM/PdM/CBM/RCM/RAM*

Ref Fig 2.1 for comparison of reactive (RM), preventive (PM), predictive/condition-based (PdM /CBM), and reliability-centered (RCM) maintenance and reliability, availability, maintainability (RAM).

For those in the mission-critical industry, availability is a must. A proper maintenance and reliability program can be the difference between whether or not, say, a hospital stays open during a crisis. By utilizing RAM, operators of a critical-care or government facility that has had trouble keeping up with repairs or is plagued by unplanned outages may finally have a means of stabilizing maintenance and regaining control of availability.(SAE, SAE, NASA)

With more and more emphasis given for energy conservation programs and policies, most existing systems are being modified or redesigned with an objective of improving energy efficiency [Dr.P.V. Shouri, Dr.P.S. Sreejith,2008]. Plant availability is a critical driver for the economic performance of a plant [Dr.P.V. Shouri, Dr.P.S. Sreejith,2008] While designing the systems, often the focus is on immediate demands of the equipment, and the broader issue of how the system parameters affect the equipment is overlooked. It is important to recognize that process efficiency and reliability are equally important [Goel H.D. et.al.,2008].

Reliability can be defined as the probability that an item can perform a required function for a specified period of time under the specified operating conditions [Patrik DTO,2002,Charles EE,2002]. Reliability of an individual component in terms of failure rate can be expressed as:

$$R(t) = e^{-\int_0^t Z(t)\, dt} \qquad\qquad (1)$$

For a component with a constant failure rate, Eq. (1) reduces to

$$R(t) = e^{-\lambda t} \qquad\qquad (2)$$

Equation (2) is generally used for the calculation of component reliabilities for a given system. In reality, even though this holds good only in-between the period of infant mortality and wear-out, it is often a reasonably good assumption as this time frame is equal to almost the entire lifetime of any equipment. The constant failure rate model is widely used in the literature to reduce the computational burden of the resulting problem because the parameter MTBF which can be obtained from Equation (3) becomes time-independent in this case [Goel HD et.al.2002]

$$MTBF = \int_0^\alpha R(t)\, dt = \int_0^\alpha e^{-\lambda t} = 1/\lambda \qquad\qquad (3)$$

Similarly, MTTR, which is the average time taken to repair a failed component, can be expressed as

$$MTTR = 1/\mu \qquad\qquad (4)$$

Availability can be defined as the probability that an item will be available when required, or as the proportion of total time the item will be available for use [Charles EE,2000]. The proportion of total time that the item is available is the steady state availability. Availability is determined by the reliability and maintainability of an item. For a simple unit with a constant failure rate and a constant mean repair rate, the steady state availability can be expressed as

$$A_i = \mu / (\lambda + \mu) \tag{5}$$

Typical approaches to achieve high system reliability are:

(1) increasing the reliability of system components and

(2) using redundant components in various subsystems in the system [You PS 2005, Kuo W,2000]. The modification of an existing system with a view to improve energy efficiency should consider these factors. The change in system configuration resulting from system modification can adversely affect the system reliability. In order to determine the economic feasibility of the new proposal several methods have been suggested to perform analyses of energy conversion systems and supply information from different view points. In the area of energy investigations,especially worth mentioning are the life cycle assessment (LCA) method presented by Valero, its exergetic version ExLCA proposed by Cornelissen et al. and the thermo economic theory presented by Lazzaretto et al., Lozano and Valero and Tsatsaronis and Winhold. This was further extended to include environmental implications by Badino and Baldo. Cumulative exergy cost accounting (CExC) was proposed by Szargut, extended exergy accounting (EEA) by Sciubba, environomic theory by Von Spakovsky and Frangopoulos and emergy accounting by Odum.

Researchers at Lawrence Berkeley National Laboratory have used life cycle costing in the United States Department of Energy's rulemaking for residential central air conditioners [Lutz James,2006]. The life cycle cost consists of two main components: (1) the first cost of buying and installing equipment and (2) the operating costs summed over the lifetime of the equipment, discounted to the present.

$$\text{Life} - \text{cycle cost} = \text{Installation cost} + \frac{\sum_{n=1}^{lifetime} Operating\, Cost}{(1+i)^n} \qquad (6)$$

The approach involves comparing the total life cycle cost (LCC) of owning and operating a more efficient appliance with the LCC for a baseline design. Lutz et al. [61] presented the method used to conduct the LCC analysis and also presented the estimated change in LCC associated with more energy efficient equipment. The LCC calculated in this analysis expresses the costs of installing and operating a furnace or boiler for its lifetime starting in the year 2012 – the year a new standard took effect. The analysis also calculated the payback period for energy efficiency design options. The pay back period represents the number of years of operation required to pay for the increased efficiency features. It is the change in purchase expense due to an increased efficiency standard divided by the change in annual operating cost that results from the increased efficiency. The payback period equation is expressed as

$$\text{Payback}_{option} = \frac{Equipment\, Cost_{Option} - Equipment\, Cost_{Base}}{Operation\, Cost_{Option} - Operation\, Cost_{Base}} \qquad (7)$$

where base is the base case design and option is the design option being considered.

It is evident from the above discussions that the system valuation and pay back analysis hardly take the reliability and availability aspects into consideration. That is, it happens that, while determining the economic feasibility of the new option, reliability aspects (or loss due to unavailability) are not taken into consideration.

The value of the system can be by considering the present worth of expected future cash flows. The model takes into consideration the system availability, in addition to the other cost elements like investment cost, and maintenance as well as operating cost[42]. The cash flow model for system valuation is shown in Fig. 3. The model is based on the following assumptions:

> ➤ Process components are assumed to have a constant failure rate as well as a constant repair rate;
> ➤ Availability under consideration is steady state availability
> ➤ Interest rate is constant throughout;
> ➤ Depreciation of the plant is not considered

With reference to the cash flow model shown in Fig 2.1, the process system value can be expressed as:

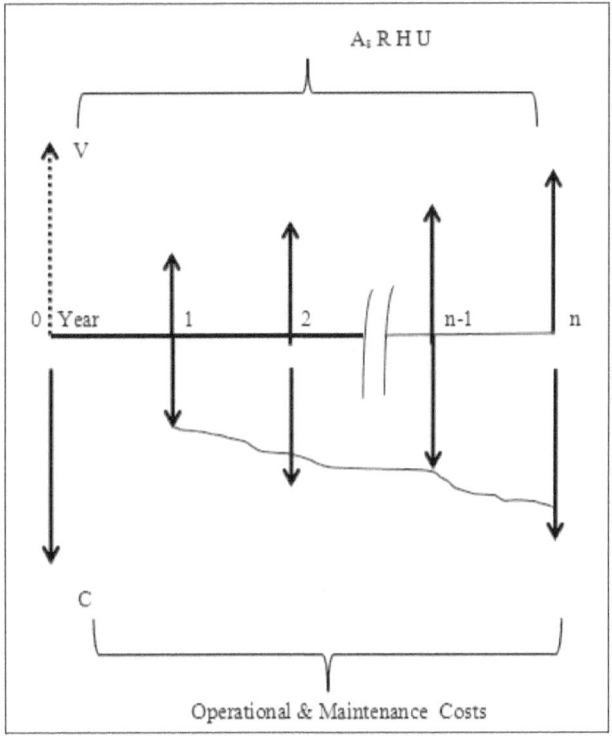

**Fig 2.2: Cash Flow Model of Process System**

$$V = A_s RHU \left( \frac{P}{A}, i, n \right) - C - A_s O_s \left[ \frac{\left[ 1 - (1+k)^n (1+i)^{-n} \right]}{(i-k)} \right] \tag{8}$$

The valuation Equation (7) can be used only for cases where i≠k and when i = k the equation will get modified as:

$$V = A_s \text{RHU} \left( \frac{P}{A}, i, n \right) - C - \left[ \frac{n A_s O_s}{(i-k)} \right] \qquad (9)$$

The quantity (P/A, i, n) in the Equation (8) is the uniform series present worth factor [61] and can be obtained as:

$$\left( \frac{P}{A}, i, n \right) = \left[ \frac{(1+i)^n - 1}{i(1+i)^n} \right] \qquad (10)$$

Whenever a process system is to be modified for energy savings, it is important to know the expected change in system value. In this case, the investment for modification, expected annual savings due to modification as well as the change in system availability has to be taken into consideration. Change in process availability results from the change in system configuration. The change in process value can be expressed as:

$$V_C = [A_M (RHU - O_M) - A_S (RHU - O_S)] (P/A, i, n) - C_m \qquad (11)$$

The payback period corresponds to the value of n that makes $V_C = 0$.

While general Calculations of reliability are based on considerations of the initial failure mode, which may be termed as "infant" mortality (decreasing failure rates the with time) or wear out mode (i.e increasing failure rates then with time). [Dr. P.V.Shouri and Jose K Jacob, 2010].

Key parameters describing reliability are [Dr. P.V.Shouri and Jose K Jacob, 2010]

- ➢ mean time to failure,
- ➢ mean time between /before repairs,
- ➢ mean life of components,
- ➢ failure rate and
- ➢ the maximum number of failures in a specific time interval.

Reliability [Dennis J Wilkins, 2002] specialists often describe the lifetime of a population of products using a graphical representation called the bathtub curve. The bathtub curve consists of three periods: an infant mortality period with a decreasing failure rate followed by a normal life period (also known as "useful life") with a low, relatively constant failure rate and concluding with a wear-out period that exhibits an increasing failure rate. This article provides an overview of how infant mortality, normal life failures and wear-out modes combine to create the overall product failure distributions. It describes methods to reduce failures at each stage of product life and shows how burn-in, when appropriate, can significantly reduce operational failure rate by screening out infant mortality failures.

The bathtub curve, [Dennis J. Wilkins,2002] displayed in Figure 2.3 below, does *not* depict the failure rate of a single item, but describes the relative failure rate of an entire population of products over time. Some individual units will fail relatively early (infant mortality failures), others (we hope most) will last until wear-out, and some will fail during the relatively long period typically called normal life. Failures during infant mortality are *highly undesirable* and are always caused by defects and blunders: material defects, design blunders, errors in assembly, etc. Normal life failures are normally considered to be random cases of "stress exceeding strength." However, as we'll see, many failures often considered normal life failures are actually infant mortality failures. Wear-out is a fact of life due to fatigue or depletion of materials (such as lubrication depletion in bearings). A product's useful life is limited by its shortest-lived component.

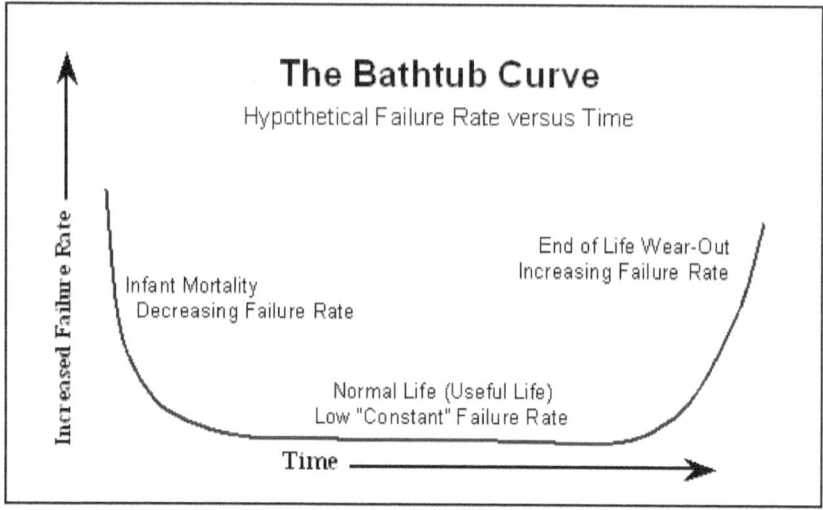

*Fig 2.3: The Bathtub Curve*

Note that the bathtub curve is typically used as a visual model to illustrate the three key periods of product failure and not calibrated to depict a graph of the expected behavior for a particular product family. It is rare to have enough short-term and long-term failure information to actually model a population of products with a calibrated bathtub curve.

Also note that the actual time periods for these three characteristic failure distributions can vary greatly. Infant mortality does not mean "products that fail within 90 days" or any other defined time period. Infant mortality is the time over which the failure rate of a product is decreasing, and may last for years. Conversely, wear-out will not always happen long after the expected product life. It is a period when the failure rate is increasing, and has been observed in products after just a few months of use. This, of course, is a disaster from a warranty standpoint!

We are interested in the characteristics illustrated by the entire bathtub curve. The infant mortality period is a time when the failure rate is dropping, but is undesirable because a significant number of failures occur in a short time, causing early customer dissatisfaction and warranty expense. Theoretically, the failures during normal life occur at random but with a relatively constant rate when measured over a long period of time. Because these failures may incur warranty expense or create service support costs, we want the bottom of the bathtub to be as low as possible. And we don't want any wear-out failures to occur during the expected useful lifetime of the product.

### Infant Mortality What Causes It and What to Do About It?

From a customer satisfaction viewpoint, infant mortalities are unacceptable. They cause "dead-on-arrival" products and undermine customer confidence. They are caused by defects designed into or built into a product. Therefore, to avoid infant mortalities, the product manufacturer must determine methods to eliminate the defects. Appropriate specifications, adequate design tolerance and sufficient component de-rating can help, and should always be used, but even the best design intent can fail to cover all possible interactions of components in operation. In addition to the best design approaches, stress testing should be started at the earliest development phases and used to evaluate design weaknesses and uncover specific assembly and materials problems. Tests like these are called HALT (Highly Accelerated Life Test) or HAST (Highly Accelerated Stress Test) and should be applied, with increasing stress levels as needed, until failures are precipitated. The failures should be investigated and design improvements should be made to improve product robustness. Such an approach can help to eliminate design and material defects that would otherwise show up with product failures in the field.

After manufacturing of a product begins, a stress test can still be valuable. There are two distinct uses for stress testing in production. One purpose (often called HASA, Highly Accelerated Stress Audit) is to identify defects caused by assembly or material variations that can lead to failure and to take action to remove the root causes of these defects. The other purpose (often called burn-in) is to use stress tests as an ongoing 100% screen to weed out defects in a product where the root causes cannot be eliminated.

The first approach, eliminating root causes, is generally the best approach and can significantly reduce infant mortalities. It is usually most cost-effective to run 100% stress screens only for early production, then reduce the screen to an audit (or entirely eliminate it) as root causes are identified, the process/design is corrected and significant problems are removed. Unfortunately, some companies put 100% burn-in processes in place and keep using them, addressing the symptoms rather than identifying the root causes. They just keep scrapping and/or reworking the same defects over and over. For most products, this is not effective from a cost standpoint or from a reliability improvement standpoint.

There is a class of products where on-going 100% burn-in has proven to be effective. This is with technology that is "state-of-the-art," such as leading edge semiconductor chips. There are bulk defects in silicon and minute fabrication variances that cannot be designed out with the current state of technology. These defects can cause some parts to fail very early relative to the majority of the population. Burn-in can be an effective way to screen out these weak parts. This will be addressed later in this article.

## A Quantitative Look at Infant Mortality Failures Using the Weibull Distribution

The Weibull distribution is a very flexible life distribution model that can be used to characterize failure distributions in all three phases of the bathtub curve. The basic Weibull distribution has two parameters, a shape parameter, often termed beta ($\beta$), and a scale parameter, often termed eta ($\eta$). The scale parameter, eta, determines when, in time, a given portion of the population will fail, *i.e.* 63.2%. The shape parameter, beta, is the key feature of the Weibull distribution that enables it to be applied to any phase of the bathtub curve. A beta less than 1 models a failure rate that decreases with time, as in the infant mortality period. A beta equal to 1 models a constant failure rate, as in the normal life period. And a beta greater than 1 models an increasing failure rate, as during wear-out. There are several ways to view this distribution, including probability plots, survival plots and failure rate versus time plots. The bathtub curve is a failure rate vs. time plot.

Typical infant mortality distributions for state-of-the-art semiconductor chips follow a Weibull model with a beta in the range of 0.2 to 0.6. If such a distribution is viewed in terms of failure rate versus time, it looks like the plot in Figure 2.4

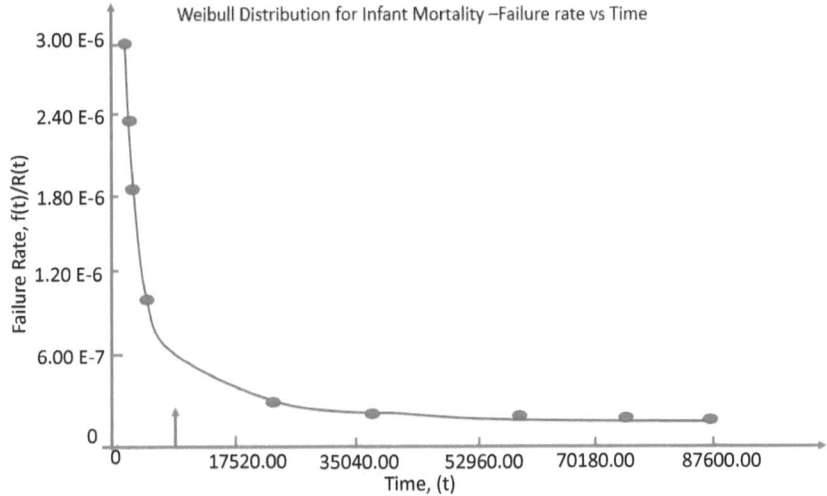

*Fig 2.4: Infant Mortality Curve - Failure Rate vs. Time*

This plot shows ten years (87,600 hours) of time on the x-axis with failure rate on the y-axis. It looks a lot like the infant mortality and normal life portions of the bathtub curve in Figure 2.3, but this curve models only infant mortality (decreasing failure rate). Dots on this plot represent failure times typical of an infant mortality with Weibull beta = 0.2. As you can see, there are 27 failures before one year, and only 6 failures from one to ten years. People observing this curve, and the failure points plotted, could not be blamed for thinking it represents both infant mortality failures (in the first year or so), and normal life failures after that. But these are only infant mortality failures - all the way out to ten years!

This plot shows the distribution for a beta value typical of complex, high-density integrated circuits (VLSI or Very Large Scale Integrated circuits). Parts such as CPUs, interface controller and video processing chips often exhibit this kind of failure distribution over time. A look at this plot shows that if you could run these parts for the equivalent of three years and discard the failed parts, the reliability of the surviving parts would be much higher out to ten years. In fact, until a wear-out mode occurs, the reliability would continue to improve over time. If there are mechanisms that can produce normal life failures (theoretically a constant failure rate) mixed in with the defects that cause the infant mortalities shown above, burn-in can still provide significant improvement as long as the constant failure rate is relatively low.

### Burn-In for Leading Edge Technologies

To see how burn-in can improve the reliability of high tech parts, we'll use a chart that looks somewhat like the failure rate vs time curve in Figure 2.4, but is more useful. This is a survival plot that directly shows how many units from a population have survived to a given time. Figure 2.5 is a plot for a typical VLSI process with a small "weak" sub-population (defective parts that will fail as infant mortalities) and a larger sub-population of parts that will fail randomly at a very low rate over the normal operating life. The x-axis scale is in years of use (zero to 100 years!) and the y-axis is percent of parts still operating to spec (starting at 100% and dropping to 50%).

Figure 2.4 shows that, of the failures that occur in the first 20 years (about 4%), most failures occur in the first year or so, just like we observed in the infant mortality example above. Because there is a low level, constant failure rate, this plot shows failures continuing for a hundred years. Of course, there could be a wear-out mode that comes into play before a hundred years has elapsed, but no wear-out distribution is considered here. Electronic components, unlike mechanical assemblies, rarely have wear-out mechanisms that are significant before many decades of operation.

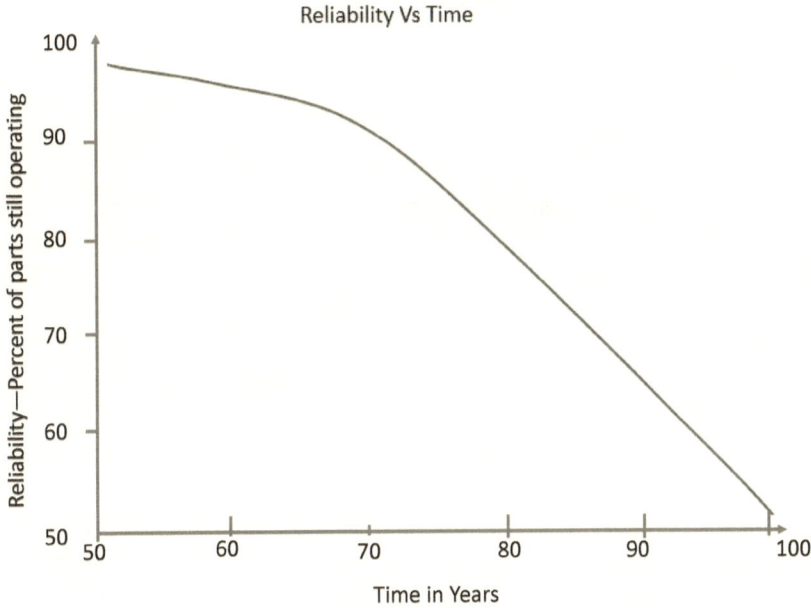

Reliability Vs Time

*Fig 2.5: Mixed Infant Mortality and Normal Life Survival Plot*

We're not really [Dennis J. Wilkins, 2002] interested in the failures much beyond ten years, so let's look at this same model for only the first ten years. In Figure 2.6, we have included sample failure points from the simulation model used to create the plot. These enable us to view which population (infant mortality or normal life) the failure came from.

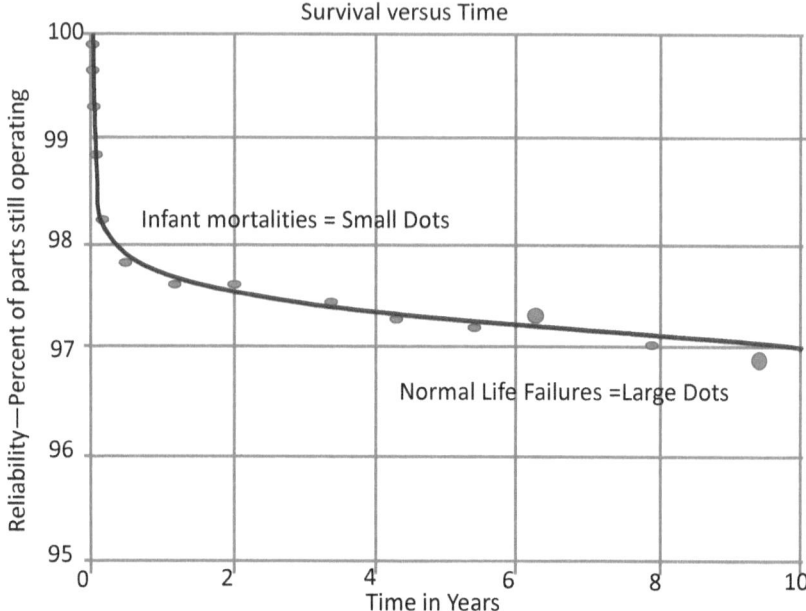

**Fig 2.6: Mixed Infant Mortality and Normal Life Failures**

We see that the [Dennis J. Wilkins,2002] in Figure 2.6 looks like the early life and normal life portions of the bathtub curve, and in fact includes both distributions. We see that over 2% of the units fail in the first year, but it takes ten years for 3% to fail. In actuality, there are still "infant" mortalities occurring well beyond ten years in this model, but at an ever-decreasing rate. In fact, in the ten year span of this model there would be very few normal life failures. Only two failures (~5% of all failures) in this example (large blue dots) come from the normal life failure population. About 95% of the failures plotted above (small red dots) are infant mortality failures! This is what the integrated circuits (IC) industry has observed with complex solid-state devices. Even after ten years of operation the primary failure cause for ICs is still infant mortality. In other words, failures are still driven primarily by defects.

In such cases, burn-in can help. In the plot [Dennis J. Wilkins,2002] above you can see that if you could get three years of operation on this part before you shipped it, you would have screened out over 80% (2% divided by 3%) of the parts that would fail in ten years. So if we were to come up with a method to effectively "age" the parts the equivalent of three years and eliminate most of the infant mortalities, the remaining parts would be more reliable than the original population. Of course, the parts that go through the three-year "burn-in" would have to last an additional ten years in the field, for a total of thirteen years. Let's see what this looks like in Figure 2.7.

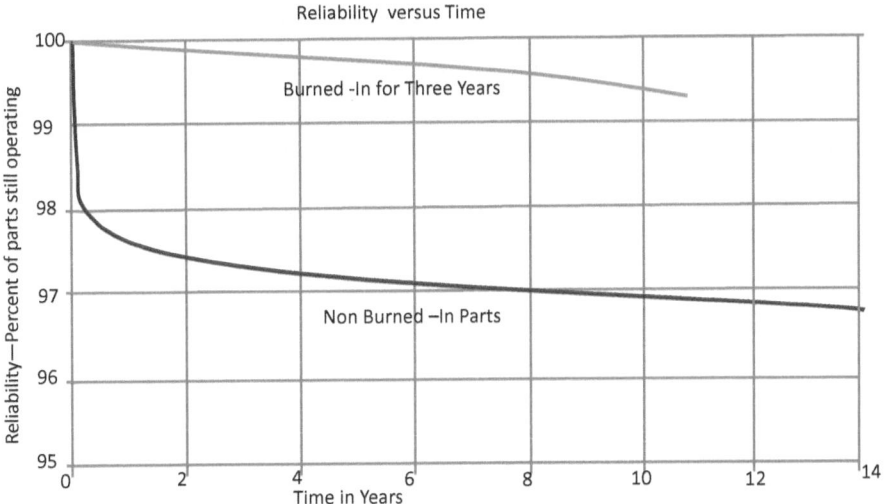

*Fig 2.7 : Comparison of Failures from Raw and Burned-in Parts*

Above, we see fourteen years[Dennis J. Wilkins,2002] of failure distribution for the original parts (not burned-in) and eleven years of expected failure distribution for parts that received three years of burn-in. In this example, the total cumulative failures between three years and thirteen years for the original parts (or from zero to ten years for burned-in parts) is about 0.6%. Without burn-in, the first ten years would have had about 3% cumulative failures. This is about a five times reduction in cumulative failures by using burn-in, or in terms of a change, we would have about 2% fewer cumulative failures in ten years with burn-in if a dominant infant mortality failure mode exists. Note that in the first year or two, the relative improvement in reliability is even greater. At two years, only about 0.1% failures are expected after burn-in but almost 2% without burn-in; a ratio of almost 25:1!

In reality, manufacturers don't have two to three years to spend on burn-in. They need an accelerated stress test. In the IC industry there are usually two stresses that are used to accelerate the effective time of burn-in: temperature and voltage. Increased temperature (relative to normal operating temperatures) can provide an acceleration of tens of times (10x to 30x is typical). Increased voltages [Dennis J. Wilkins,2002] (relative to normal operating levels) can provide even higher acceleration factors on many types of ICs. Combined acceleration factors in the range of 1000:1, or more, are typical for many IC burn-in processes. Therefore, burn-in times of tens of hours can provide effective operating times of one to five years, significantly reducing the proportion of parts with infant mortality defects.

What if we try burn-in on a product [Dennis J. Wilkins,2002] with no dominant infant mortality problems? The survival plot for an assembly with a 1% per year "constant" failure rate (normal life period) is shown below in Figure 2.8.

It's pretty easy to see that burn-in for two years [Dennis J. Wilkins,2002] would find ~2% failures, but operation for an additional two years would find another ~2%. At ten years, we would have found about 10%. Note, the line is not really a straight line because a constant failure rate (equivalent to the normal life part of the bathtub) acts on the remaining population and the remaining population is decreasing as units fail. Looking at the [62] same burn-in conditions as in the last example, if we were to provide three years of operation on these parts and then use them for an additional ten years, what results would we have? The cumulative failures of the units that passed this screen would be very close to 9.5%. Without burn-in, the cumulative failures in ten years would be the same, about 9.5%. There is no advantage to burn-in with a constant (normal life) failure rate.

It should be obvious that burn-in of an assembly that is failing due to a wear-out failure mode (failure rate increasing with time) will actually yield assemblies that are worse than units that did not go through burn-in. This is simply because the probability of failure is increasing for every hour the parts run. Adding operating time simply increases the possibility of a failure in any future period of time!

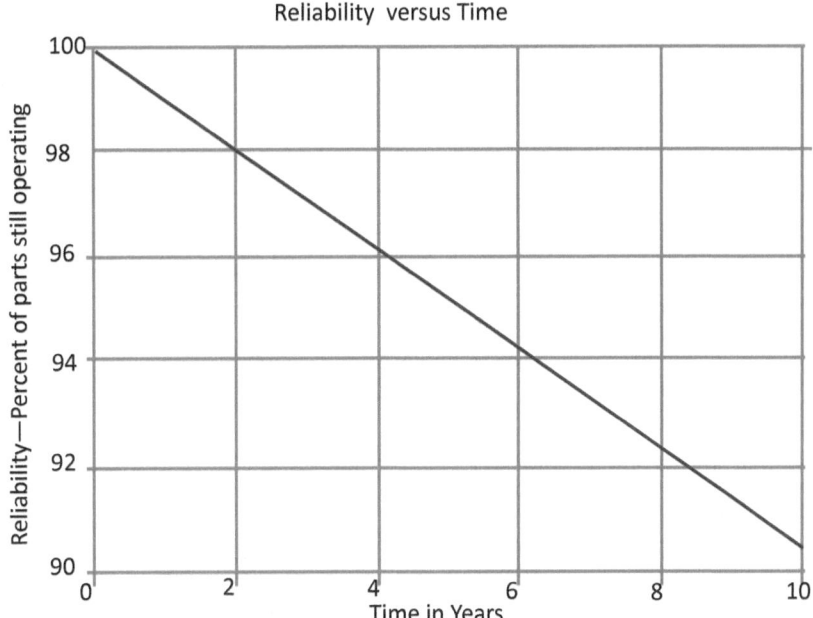

Fig 2.8 : Survival Plot for Constant Failure Rate

Reliabilities in power plants is affected by operating periods that is between scheduled outages, budget periods and peak production periods. Measuring the reliabilities of plant and equipment by quantifying the annual cost of unreliability incurred by the facility puts reliability into a business context.[Dr.Jose K Jacob, Dr.P.V.Shouri,2010]

Higher plant reliability reduces equipment failure costs where as failure decreases production and limits gross profits. [Dr.Jose K Jacob, Dr.P.V.Shouri,2010]

Reliability Engineering provides the theoretical and practical tools where by the probability and capability of parts and components, products, subsystems and systems to perform their required functions without failure for desired periods of specified environments. [Dr.Jose K Jacob, Dr.P.V.Shouri,2010]

The equation for change in process value can be used to study the impact of system modification on system value and a positive value for Vc is desirable. The equation for change in process value can be used to study the impact of system modification on system value and a positive value for Vc is desirable. The equation can also be used to study the effect of variation of operating parameters on the system value. A positive value for Vc implies that the cost of modification can be recovered. On the other hand, a negative value for $V_C$ implies that the modification will only result in decreasing the earnings of the system with the passage of time.

## 2.3 Process System Value

The value of the system is determined by considering the present worth of expected future cash flows. The cash flow model developed [Dr.P.V.Shouri,Dr.P.S.Sreejith,2008]for system valuation is shown in Fig 2.2.Whenever a process system is to be modified for energy savings, it is important to know the expected change in system value. In this case, the investment for modification and the expected annual savings due to modification, as well as the change in system availability, have to be taken into consideration. Change in process availability results from change in system configuration. The equation for change in process value can be used to study the impact of system modification on system value and a positive value for VC is desirable. The equation can also be used to study the effect of variation of operating parameters on the system value. [Dr.P.V.Shouri,Dr.P.S.Sreejith,2008]

## 2.4 Break Even Availability

A positive value for $V_C$ implies that the cost of modification can be recovered, and the equation can be used to determine the pay back period. On the other hand, a negative value for $V_C$ implies that the modification will only result in decreasing the earnings of the system with the passage of time. In this case, the equation can be used to calculate the break even availability of the modified system, for a given payback period. The modified system availability should be greater than this break even availability for $V_C$ to be positive. The break even availability is the value of $A_m$ corresponding to $V_C = 0$, at a given payback period. The system valuation model can be used to develop an algorithm for allocation of component reliabilities of the modified system based on the break even system availability. Reliability engineers are often called upon to make decisions as to whether to improve a certain component or components in order to achieve the minimum required system reliability. It happens that even by raising the individual component reliability to a hypothetical value of 1, the overall system reliability goal will not be met by improving the reliability of just one component. This requires that the reliability goal be apportioned among the system components, and an algorithm is developed for this purpose.

[Dr.P.V.Shouri,Dr.P.S.Sreejith,2008]

## 2.5 Reliability Allocation in System Modification

The process by which the failure allowance for a system is allocated in some logical manner among its sub-systems and elements is termed reliability allocation.

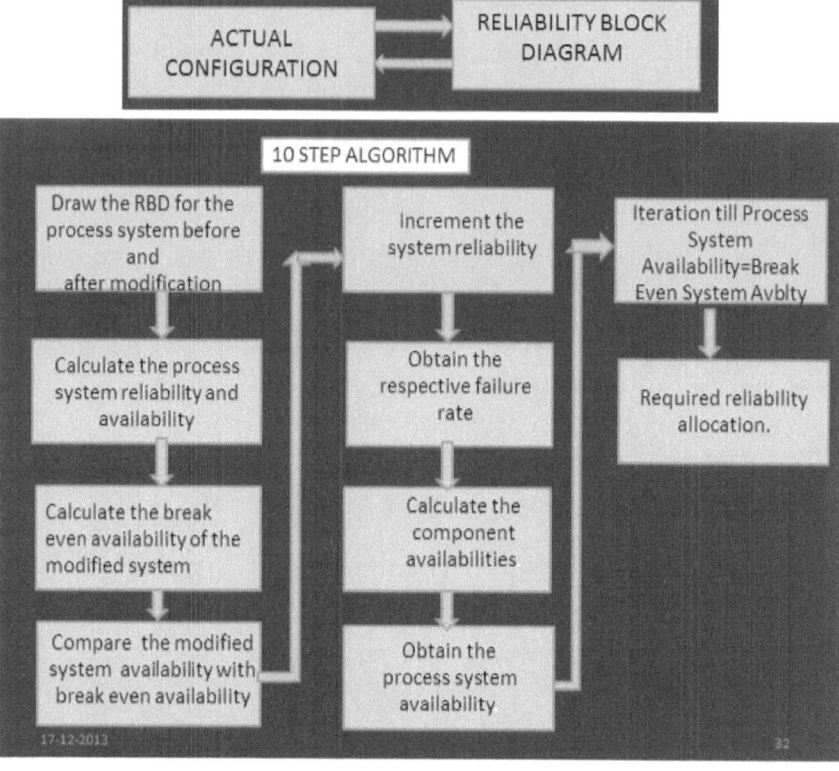

*Fig 2.9 : Ten Step Algorithm for Reliability Allocation*

## 2.6 Energy Analysis of the process System

The process plants that are operated on continuous basis consume large quantities of energy [65].Energy analysis intend to analyze the process system components separately and to identify and quantify the sites having largest energy losses at different loads.It is observed that a detailed energy analysis is not done even in many process industries. Studies of energy and exergy analyses for power generation systems are of scientific interest and also essential for the efficient utilization of energy resources. Efficiency is one of the most frequently used terms in thermodynamics, and it indicates how well an energy conversion or process is accomplished. Efficiency is also one of the most frequently misused terms in thermodynamics and is often a source of misunderstanding. This is because efficiency is often used without being properly defined first. Efficiency traditionally has been primarily defined based on the first law (i.e., energy). This efficiency was based on the specific heat input to the steam. Energy analysis is done by performing energy balance of the power plant main components at various loads. Nonetheless, efficiencies based on energy can often be non-intuitive or even misleading, in part because it does not provide a measure of ideality. In addition, losses of energy can be large quantity while it is thermodynamically insignificant due to its low quality.

The First Law deals with the amounts of energy of various forms transferred between the system and its surroundings and with the changes in the energy stored in the system. It treats work and heat interactions as equivalent forms of energy in transit and offers no indication about the possibility of a spontaneous process proceeding in a certain direction. The first law places no restriction on the direction of a process, but satisfying the first law does not ensure that the process can actually occur. This inadequacy of the first law to identify whether a process can take place is remedied by introducing another general principle, the second law of thermodynamics [Sarang J. Gulhanel et. al. 2013]

In an open flow system there are three types of energy transfer across the control surface namely working transfer, heat transfer, and energy associated with mass transfer and/or flow. The first law of thermodynamics or energy balance for the steady flow process. of an open system is given by

$$\sum \dot{Q}_k + \dot{m} \left( h_i + \frac{C_i{}^2}{2} + g\, Z_i \right) = \dot{m} \left( h_o + \frac{C_o{}^2}{2} + g\, Z_o \right) + \dot{W}$$

where $Q_k$ is the heat transfer to system from source at temperature $T_k$, and W is the network developed by the system. The other notations C is the bulk velocity of the working fluid, Z, is the altitude of the stream above the sea level, g is the specific gravitational force. The energy or first law efficiency of a system and/or system component is defined as the ratio of energy output to the energy input to system/component i.e.

$$⊠_I = \text{Desired output energy /Input energy supplied}$$

## 2.7 Second Law Efficiency Analysis of the Process System

**Second Law efficiency Analysis** evaluates system performance in converting input exergy (fuel exergy) into exergy associated with the delivered products.It is observed that a detailed energy analysis in not done even in many process industries. Potential second law efficiency, Assesses the potential additional exergy efficiency deriving from exploiting the outlet flows that exist as streams but are not considered as useful products and effectively used. These products are normally useful only if particular conditions occur (consider, for example, the heat released with flue gases when low temperature heat is not needed nearby).Studies of energy and exergy analyses for power generation systems are of scientific interest and also essential for the efficient utilization of energy resources. For this reason, the exergy analysis has drawn much attention by scientists and system designers in recent years [A Rashad,A El.Maihey,2009].

Efficiency traditionally has been primarily defined based on the first law (i.e., energy). In recent decades, exergy analysis has found increasingly widespread acceptance as a useful tool in the design, assessment, optimization and improvement of energy systems [A Rashad,A El.Maihey,2009].

Determining exergy efficiencies for an overall system and/or the individual components making up the system constitutes a major part of exergy analysis. A comprehensive analysis of a thermodynamic system includes both energy and exergy analyses in order to obtain a more complete picture of system behaviour [A Rashad,A El.Maihey,2009].

Exergy is a generic term for a group of concepts that define the maximum possible work potential of a system,a stream of matter and/or heat interaction ;the state of the (conceptual) environment being used as the datum state. In an open flow system there are three types of energy transfer across the control surface namely working transfer, heat transfer,and energy associated with mass transfer and/or flow. The work transfer is equivalent to the maximum work, which can be obtained from that form of energy. The exergy of heat transfer Q from the control surface at temperature T is determined from maximum rate of conversion of thermal energy to work $W_{max.}$ is given by:

$$W_{max} = \psi_Q = Q\left(1 - \frac{T0}{T}\right)$$

Exergy of steady flow stream of matter is the sum of kinetic, potential and physical exergy. The kinetic and potential energy are almost equivalent to exergy.The physical specific exergy $\Psi_i$ and $\Psi_o$ depends on initial state of matter and environmental state. Energy analysis is based on the first law of thermodynamics,which is related to the conservation of energy.Second law analysis is a method that uses the conservation of mass and degradation of the quality of energy along with the entropy generation in the analysis. [S.C. Kaushik et. Al. 2011]

Second law analysis [S.C. Kaushik et. Al.,2011] is a method that uses the conservation of mass and degradation of the quality of energy along with the entropy generation in the analysis design and improvement of energy systems. Exergy analysis is a useful method to complement but not to replace energy analysis. The exergy flow for steady flow process of an open system is given by

$$\sum\left(1 - \frac{T0}{T}\right)Q_k + \sum_{in}\dot{m}\psi i = \psi_w + \sum_{out}\dot{m}\psi o + I_{destroyed°;}$$
$$\Psi \dot{m}\left[(h^0 - h^0{}_o)\right] - T_0(s-s_0),\quad h^0$$
$$= h + [C^2/2] + g\,Z,\quad I_{destroyed} = T_0\left[\dot{S}_{gen}\right]$$

where $\Psi_i$ and $\Psi_o$ are exergy associated with mass inflow and outflows are respectively, $\Psi_w$ is useful work done on/by system, $I_{destroyed}$ is irreversibility of process and $h_0$ is the methalpy as summation of enthalpy, kinetic energy and potential energy. The other notations C is the bulk velocity of the working fluid, Z is the altitude of the stream above the sealevel,g is the specific gravitational force. The irreversibility [S.C. Kaushik et. Al. 2011]

may be due to heat transfer through finite temperature difference,mixing of fluids at different temperature and mechanical friction.Exergy analysis is an effective means,to pinpoint losses due to irreversibility in a realsituation. The second law efficiency is defined as

$\boxtimes_{II}$ = Exergy output /Exergy input.

To analyze the possible realistic performance, a detailed exergy analysis of the coal fired thermal power plant has been carried out by ignoring the kinetic and potential energy change. For steady state flow the exergy balance for a thermal system is given as below

$$\Psi_w = \sum_{k=1}^{n}\left(1 - \frac{T0}{T}\right)Q_k + \sum_{k=1}^{r}[(\dot{m}\,\Psi)_i - (\dot{m}\,\Psi)_o]_k - T0\,[\dot{S}_{gen}]$$

where $\Psi w$ represents the useful work done and/or by the system, the first term on the right hand side $[(1-T_0/T_k)Q_k]$ represents the exergy summation supplied through heat transfer,while changes in the exergy summation of the working fluid is represented by the second term where i and o refers the inlet and outlet states. On the other hand,the exergy distraction and/or the irreversibility in the system is given by the last term on the right hand side,$[T_0\,\dot{S}_{gen}]$. The other notations such as, Q is the heat transfer rate, m is the mass flow rate of the working fluid, is the exergy flow rate per unit mass, $S_{gen}$ is the entropy generation rate, $T_0$ is the ambient air temperature, $T_k$ is the temperature of the heat source/sink at which the heat is transferred/rejected.

$$\eta_{II} = \frac{(Actual\ Thermal\ Efficiency\ )}{(Maximum\ possible\ (reversible)thermal\ efficiency)}$$

$$= \frac{Exergy\ output}{Exergy\ input}$$

$$Q° - W° = \sum m°e\ he - \sum m°i\ hi$$

$$X°\ heat - X° = \sum m°e\ \Psi e - \sum m°i\ \Psi i$$

Where the net exergy transfer by heat ($X°$ heat ) at température T is given by

$$X°\ heat = \sum(1-\frac{T0}{T})Q°$$

And the specific exergy is given by

$$\Psi = h-h_{o} - T_{o}(s-s_{o})$$

Then the total exergy rate associated with a fluid stream becomes

$$X° = m°\ \Psi = \dot{m}\ [h-h_{o} - T_{o}(s-s_{o})]$$

*Fig 2.10 : Expressions for Exergy Rate*

| | EXERGY DESTRUCTION RATE | 2nd Law Efficiency ($\eta II$) |
|---|---|---|
| PUMPS | $I°_{pump} = X°_{in} - X°_{out} + W°_{pumps}$ | $\eta II.pump = 1- \dfrac{I°pump}{W°\ pump}$ |
| HEATERS | $I°_{heater} = X°_{in} - X°_{out}$ | $\eta II.heater = 1- \dfrac{I°heater}{X°\ in}$ |
| TURBINE | $I°_{turbine} = X°_{in} - X°_{out} - W°_{el}$ | $\eta II.heater = 1- \dfrac{I°turbine}{X°\ in- X°\ out}$ |
| CONDENSER | $I°_{turbine} = X°_{in} - X°_{out} + W°_{f}$ | $\eta II.condenser = 1- \dfrac{X°\ out}{X°\ in +W°\ f}$ |
| CYCLE COMPONENTS | $I°\ cycle = \sum_{all\ components} I°$ | $\eta II.cycle = 1- \dfrac{W°\ net\ out}{X\ fuel}$ |

*Fig 2.11: Exergy Destruction Rate and Second Law Efficiency*

## 2.8 LNG Value Chain

In the LNG value chain, liquefaction is the most critical part of the processing chain. When designing an onshore LNG plant—especially the liquefaction section—it is important to consider critical design parameters. [http://www.gasprocessingnews.com/features/201404/consider-factors-affecting-onshore-lng-plant-design.aspx]

**Composition of feed and export market.** The composition and variability of the feed gas are essential parameters in the design of an LNG plant. The contaminants (acid gases, water, mercury and sulfurous components) contained in the gas determine the type and complexity of the plant's preprocessing section.

The heavy hydrocarbons content influences the choice of the NGL recovery section, the fractionation technology and the complexity of the gas receiving section (including the slug catcher, stabilization process and other components). If the heavy hydrocarbons content is high, more energy will be consumed in the NGL recovery section to process the higher flow of liquid hydrocarbons and extract products to specification.

The sizing of a plant based on the heaviest input composition must be carefully considered, keeping in mind that oversized fractionation columns may not operate at the lower flowrates associated with a lighter feed gas composition. Feed gas normally contains three to six different cases—i.e., rich composition, lean composition and base composition, with variation in ambient temperature.

Every country has individual specifications for the heating value and composition of the gas it purchases. For example, gas with a heating value of less than 1,065 British thermal units per standard cubic foot (Btu/scf) is suitable for the US and UK markets, whereas this value is too low for the Asian market, which requires gas to have a heating value greater than 1,090 Btu/scf. In Europe, the requirement is between 990 Btu/scf and 1,160 Btu/scf.

A gas interchangeability index, the Wobbe Index, is also used in Europe. The Wobbe Index is defined as the ratio of higher heating value to the square root of gas-specific gravity (relative to air), and it is often more stringent than the heating value specification. Inert gases like helium (He) and nitrogen ($N_2$) decide the post-liquefaction processes—i.e., the He/$N_2$ recovery section. Very low (< 1%) $N_2$ content does not require any treatment for $N_2$ and is acceptable in LNG, whereas moderate to high $N_2$ content requires $N_2$ stripping or the inclusion of an $N_2$ recovery section.

LNG plants that aim to meet the needs of more than one market must have a flexible NGL recovery unit that is equipped with devices suitable for re-injecting heavy components into the gas to be liquefied.

**Technology selection.** The technology selection is determined by the size of the plant and the capacity of the gas reservoir. A proprietary, propane-precooled mixed-refrigerant (MR) process is used when the baseload capacity is between 4 million tons per year (MMtpy) and 4.5 MMtpy. In this process, precooling is done by propane, whereas liquefaction and subcooling duty is provided by an MR. Process capacity is limited due to refrigerant compressor driver power. For increased capacity, liquefaction duty is provided by the MR process, and a nitrogen-expander loop is added to provide subcooling duty. This setup reduces the load on the MR compressor driver.

Another propane MR process is used, with capacities up to 3 MMtpy. For increased capacity, MR in series with a varied composition is used to provide precooling, liquefaction and subcooling duty.

One of the key elements of the technology is the heat exchanger equipment for liquefaction—i.e., the coil-wound heat exchanger (CWHE), the cold box, etc. Only a few vendors offer CWHEs, while many offer cold box technology.

**Ambient conditions.** For the liquefaction section, ambient conditions (air temperature, humidity, ambient pressure, wind direction, etc.) influence the driver's powering of rotating equipment (i.e., gas turbine) and air cooler performance. The choice of liquefaction technology and the selection of the drivers depend on the environmental parameters related to the geographical position of the plant.

As the air temperature increases, the efficiency of the turbine decreases, with a consequent reduction in plant production due to the decrease in available turbine power. In particular, aeroderivative turbines are much more sensitive to air temperature than are industrial turbines. The reduction in power is approximately 0.7% per °C increase in temperature for gas turbines, and for aeroderivative turbines, the available power decreases by approximately 1.1% per °C increase in temperature.

Although low temperatures are favorable for plant production, very low temperatures have been found to negatively influence precooling cycles. In many processes, precooling is provided by propane. In this case, the precooling temperature is limited (–30°C to –35°C) by pure propane (i.e., an adjustment in composition is not possible), and propane must be above atmospheric pressure throughout the loop.

As feed and other refrigerants are cooled by ambient air more frequently, the loads on the propane compressor decrease. After a point, the compressor goes into partial recycle mode to maintain its operation. This increases specific energy used by the propane compressor. Therefore, in cold climates, dual-mixed-refrigerant (DMR) technology is preferred since it permits changes in the composition of the refrigerant when the air temperature changes.

Atmospheric pressure has little impact on technology selection and plant production. However, gas turbine power increases as atmospheric pressure increases.

The effect of air humidity on turbine power is not very marked, and, therefore, the corresponding change in production at the plant is not very noticeable. However, at higher capacities, the turbine effect is noticeable. The air humidity effect is the result of the control system's approximation of the firing temperature used on gas turbines. Single-shaft turbines that use turbine exhaust temperature determined by the compressor pressure ratio to the approximate firing temperature will reduce power as a result of increased ambient humidity. The control system is set to follow the inlet air temperature function.

In contrast, the control system on aero derivatives uses unbiased gas generator discharge temperature to approximate firing temperature.

Since the gas generator is a double- or triple-shaft turbine, it can operate at different speeds from the power turbine, and the power will increase as fuel is added to raise the humid air to the allowable temperature. This fuel increase will raise the gas generator speed and compensate for the loss in air density.[1]

Humidity facilitates heat exchange in air-based heat exchangers, since it improves the film coefficient. The effect of the strength and direction of the wind should also be considered, and hot air circulation effect should be taken into account when designing equipment, especially air coolers.

**Operating pressure.** The energy efficiency of liquefaction depends on the liquefaction operating pressure. High feed gas pressures require less power for liquefaction. The effect of liquefaction inlet pressure on liquefaction duty to cool it from an initial temperature of 40°C to –155°C is shown in **Fig. 2.12.**

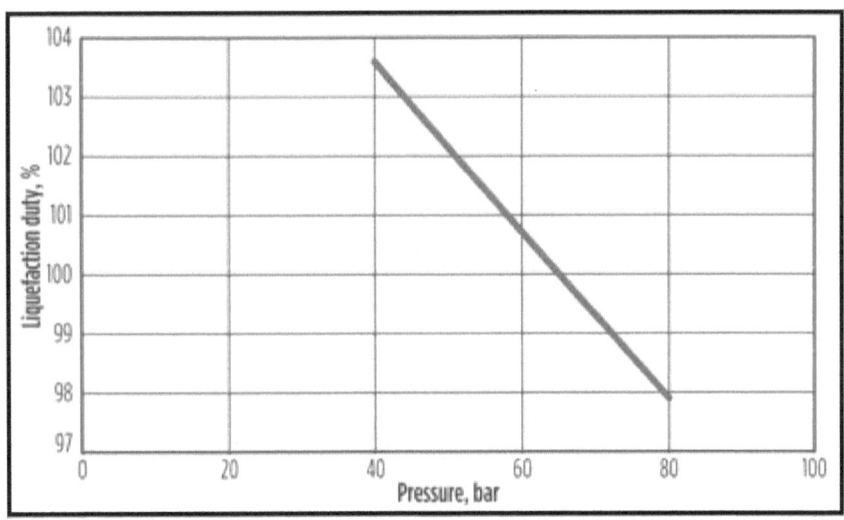

*Fig 2.12 Variation in liquefaction duty with pressure.*

A typical LNG composition of 93% methane, 5% ethane, 1% propane and 1% $N_2$ is assumed. A reference pressure of 65 bar is used for the reference duty value. The considered pressure range is 40 bar–80 bar. **Fig. 2.13** shows a pressure enthalpy diagram of LNG with the same composition. As shown, $\Delta H$ is the difference in enthalpy due to the pressure variation from 40 bar to 80 bar.

High operating pressures add complexities and costs to LNG plants, counteracting the advantages of reduced liquefaction duty. High operating pressures may increase the costs of acid gas removal, mercury removal and dehydration, and make the removal of heavy hydrocarbons more complex. The optimum operating pressure is determined by balancing these various functions.

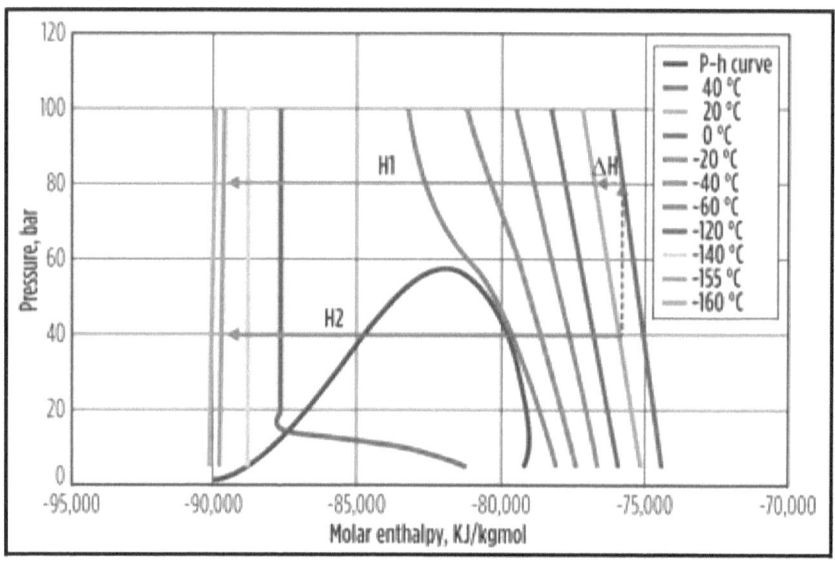

*Fig 2.13 Pressure enthalpy diagram.*

**Choice of cooling media.** The two most commonly used refrigerants are water and air. The major factor that influences the choice of cooling media is seasonal temperature variation in water and air. The seasonal variation in water temperature is lower and more gradual compared to the variation in air temperature.

**Availability of water.** Once the availability of water near the plant is ensured, the choice must be made between direct seawater cooling and indirect seawater cooling. The use of direct seawater for cooling is the most cost-effective, safe, and process-stable. Unlike air coolers, which must operate over wide fluctuations in temperature, seawater coolers have a predictable, narrow and more stable temperature range.

The use of direct seawater requires superior materials that are difficult to source on the market (such as titanium), which makes this type of cooling a long lead item. Direct seawater, as compared to indirect seawater, offers the highest efficiency and compactness through a wider temperature approach and fewer required heat exchangers and pumps.

Today's environmental and regulatory challenges are considerably greater than those that existed during the design of the first- and second-generation LNG plants in the 1960s and 1970s. For environmental reasons, the highest permitted temperature increase for seawater is usually 5°C.

When a water-based heat exchanger is stopped, the temperature increase of the process fluid is greater than that seen when an air-based heat exchanger is interrupted. In the latter case, part of the heat exchange is provided by natural convection.

**Choice of heat transfer media.** Steam and hot oil are the two media usually used for heat transfer in an LNG plant. Steam is used if it is available; i.e., if the plant has a unit to generate it. The advantage of using steam is that it can be produced at any temperature and, therefore, heat exchange can take place at a level suitable to each user. However, due to the high pressures involved, the use of steam is considered a hazardous operation.

The use of hot oil, on the contrary, is preferable since no particular maintenance operations are required and it is not dangerous. However, the cost of the oil has an impact on the capital expenditure of the plant.

**Compressor driver.** Most of the power in the LNG plant is consumed by the refrigeration compressor. Lower driver efficiency translates into higher fuel gas demand, which leads to higher plant auto-consumption. Auto-consumption, a measure of the thermal efficiency of a plant, is the ratio of the total heating values of fuel gas to feed gas.

The driver of an LNG plant can be a steam turbine, a gas turbine, an aero derivative turbine or an electrical motor. Steam turbines are no longer used, as they require a dedicated steam/water network and have issues related to the water/steam system.

Gas turbines are widely used due to their proven experience in the LNG sector. One of the key features of gas turbines is that they are available in small to very large capacities. Large-capacity turbines are required for large LNG trains with capacities of 4 MMtpy–5 MMtpy. Gas turbine thermal efficiency is less than that of aeroderivative-type turbines. Furthermore, high-power single-shaft gas turbines cannot be started from a refrigerant compressor settle-out condition. Therefore, the entire inventory from the compressor system must be routed to an appropriate system—i.e., flaring. Large, single-shaft gas turbines also require large starter motors.

*Fig 2.14: LNG Tanker Vessel*

Aero derivative turbines are not available with very high power output; however, for larger trains, they are used in parallel arrangements. They have higher thermal efficiency and, therefore, lower fuel gas consumption. Aero derivative turbines can be started from a compressor settle-out condition as they have multiple shafts, and they do require a large motor to start.

Electric motors can also be used as a driver. These motors can negate ambient effects (e.g., air temperature variation) as power is generated at other places. The efficiency of an electric motor depends on the power-generation method since, after power generation, some efficiency is lost in transmission. For refrigerant compressor drivers in LNG plants, there is limited experience with electric motors.

**Takeaway.** Careful consideration of design elements, and the array of choices they encompass, is necessary for the successful design of an onshore LNG plant. The technology selection for the liquefaction section is of particular importance, as liquefaction is the most critical part of the processing chain. Special attention must be given to ambient conditions at the plant location, as these will affect the liquefaction technology options available to plant designers.

*Fig 2.15: LNG Storage Tank On Shore*

# CHAPTER 3

# PROBLEM FORMULATION AND UNDERLYING CONCEPTS

## 3.1. Background

The performed literature survey tells the need for incorporation of reliability,availability,energy and efficiency analysis in process system modifications and their importance and impact on the process system value and the exergoeconomic performance. During surveillance visits it is understood that many main process industries have not incorporated the parameters in process system modifications. In reality, many process industries are prone to suffer losses in process system modifications without the incorporation of them. This has made to consider to develop the book.

"Process System Value and Exergoeconomic Performance of Captive Power Plants"

## 3.2. Problem Formulation

Problem is formulated on the basis of LNG Conversion of Oil fired Boiler of 7 MW Capacity Captive power plant of a Petrochemical plant of a fertilizer industry. The major modifications are done in De-Super Heater and Flame Burner system of the 60 TPH capacity boilers.

## 1. De -Super Heater Modifications

- Change in Material Grade
- Change in diameter of De-Super Heater Header Pipe from 1inch to 2 inches to accommodate the increased steam capacity due to feed stock change.

## 2. Flame Burner System Modifications

Burner System Modifications - from config. Furnace Oil/Purge Gas/ LPG to Furnace Oil/Purge Gas/LPG/LNG

### 3.3. Underlying Concepts

- **Reliability**

Reliability is defined as the probability of a system performing its purpose adequately for a period of time intended under the operating conditions encountered. [Etienne Human,2012]

The definition can be break down into four basic parts, namely:

➢ Probability
➢ Adequate Performance
➢ Time
➢ Operating conditions

- **Availability**

Availability can be defined as the probability that an item will be available when required, or as the proportion of total time the item will be available for use. The proportion of total time that the item is available is the steady state availability. Availability deals with the duration of up-time for operations and is a measure of *how often* the system is alive and well. It is often expressed as (up-time)/(up-time + downtime) with many different variants.

- **First Law of Thermodynamics**

The First Law of Thermodynamics states that energy can be converted from one form to another with the interaction of heat, work and internal energy, but it **cannot** be created nor destroyed, under any circumstances. Mathematically, this is represented as

$$\Delta U = q + w$$

with

- $\Delta U$ is the total change in internal energy of a system,
- $q$ is the heat exchanged between a system and its surroundings, and
- $w$ is the work done by or on the system.

- **Second Law of Thermodynamics**

The Second Law of Thermodynamics states that the state of entropy of the entire universe, as an isolated system, will always increase over time. The second law also states that the changes in the entropy in the universe can never be negative and "all **spontaneous** processes produce an **increase** in the entropy of the universe".

### 3.4. Objectives

- ➤ What is the effect of system modification for improving energy efficiency on CPP system configuration?
- ➤ What is the impact of LNG Conversion modifications on reliability and availability of the captive power plant?
- ➤ What is the change in process system value as a result of modification?
- ➤ If the change in system value is negative how can it be rectified by reallocating the component availabilities?
- ➤ What is the impact of variation in fuel prices on the process system value of modifications?

> ➤ Conduct Energy analysis that intend to analyze the process system components separately and to identify and quantify the sites having largest energy losses by first law.
> ➤ Conduct Second law efficiency analysis of major captive power plant components before and after modification.

# CHAPTER 4

# SITE DATA, FIELD WORK AND RESULTS

## 4.1 Background

- ➤ Literature Survey
- ➤ Problem Formulation
- ➤ Data Collection
- ➤ System Description
- ➤ Model Development

Literature survey done and the Problem formulation are explained before.This section will be dealing mainly on Data Collection and Model Development.

## 4.2 Data Collection

The field data as well as salient features were collected from the captive power plant. There are three boilers of 60 TPH capacity. Furnace oil /fuel oil is used in the existing system for generating steam. The capacity of each boiler is 60 TPH of steam. There are two burners in each boiler with burner fittings.

Refer Table 4.1 for Burner data The relevant parameters are Fuel used, Fuel combination, Number of burners per boiler, Register size,

Atomization, Atomizing pressure, T/d, Maximum, minimum and normal oil capacity per burner, Oil pressure at burner max. and the type of gas.

### Table 4.1: Burner Data

| Burners | Units 1 and 2 | Unit 3 |
|---|---|---|
| **Fuel** | LSHS/FO &Off gas | LSHS/FO |
| **Fuel combination** | Oil + off gas (off gas to be fired only if oil flow to burner is > 250 kg/hr) | Only oil firing provision provided |
| **No: of burners per boiler** | 2(located in front wall) | 2(located in front wall) |
| **Register size** | 720 mm | 665 mm |
| **Atomisation** | Steam | Steam |
| **Atomising pressure** | 7 kg per sq.cm | 7 kg per sq. Cm |
| **T/d** | 01:04 | 01:04 |
| **Max. Oil capacity/burner** | 2530 kg/hr | 2530 kg/hr |
| **Normal oil capacity/burner** | 2300 kg/hr | 2300 kg/hr |
| **Minimum oil capacity/burner** | 632 kg/hr | 2(located in front wall) |
| **Oil pressure at burner max.** | 14.5 kg/sq.cm | 14.5 kg/sq.cm |
| **Type of gas** | Fuel gas (off gas from fertiliser plant) | N/a |

The fuels used in the existing arrangement is Fuel Oil and Off gas where as in the modified arrangement is LNG.

Refer Table 4.2 for Specification of fuel oil (furnace oil)

The parameters in the table are the Type of fuel oil/ sg, Gross Heating Value, Viscosity of fuel required at burners, Oil flow and pressure per burner at peak load and m.c.r respectively.

| TABLE 4.2 : SPECIFICATION OF FUEL OIL | | |
|---|---|---|
| **Type/sg** | Kg/hr | Heavy fuel oil/1.008 |
| **Gross heating value** | Kcal/kg | 9500 |
| **Viscosity required at burners** | 15-20-degree Celsius | 4 |
| **Oil flow per burner at peak load** | Kg/hr | 2530 |
| **Oil flow per burner at m.c.r** | Kg/hr | 2300 |
| **Oil pressure at burner for peak load** | Kg/sq.cm | 14.5 |
| **Oil pressure required at burner for m.c.r** | Kg/sq.cm | 13.5 |

The off-gas data is as per Table-4.3. The given data is analysis by weight for the content of gases Hydrogen, Methane,Oxygen, and Nitrogen.

| TABLE 4.3: SPECIFICATION FOR OFF-GAS | | |
|---|---|---|
| **Analysis by weight** | | |
| **Hydrogen** | Kg/hr | 92 |
| **Methane** | Kg/hr | 51 |
| **Oxygen** | Kg/hr | 4 |
| **Nitrogen** | Kg/hr | 2315 |
| **Fuel gas qty** | Kg/hr | 2662 |

Refer Table 4.4 for Properties of off gas. The properties mentioned are Calorific Value, Density, Gas pressure and Temperature.

| TABLE 4.4: PROPERTIES OF OFF GAS | | |
|---|---|---|
| Calorific value | K Cal/kg | 3000 |
| Density at 15 deg. Celsius | Kg/ m³ | 0.696 |
| Gas pressure at terminal | Kg/sq.cm | 10 @ 38 degree Celsius |
| Temp | Degree Celsius | 38 degree Celsius |

Refer Table 4.5 for LNG specification. The parameters that are specified are Expected pressure and temperature of LNG, Gas calorific value, Molecular weight and Specific density.

| TABLE 4.5: LNG SPECIFICATION | | |
|---|---|---|
| Expected pressure and temperature of LNG | Kg/hr | 85 bar, 0 degree celsius |
| GCV | Kcal/kg | 114800 |
| Mol.weight | Kg/k mol | 18.29 |
| Specific density | | 0.65 |

Refer Table 4.6 for Required parameters at Boiler terminal point. The required parameters are Pressure of Re gasified LNG, Temperature and Dryness.

| TABLE 4.6: REQUIRED PARAMETERS AT BOILER TERMINAL POINT | | |
|---|---|---|
| Pressure of Re-gasified LNG | Kg/Sq.cm | 4(min 3 –max 5 kg /Sq.cm |
| Temperature | Deg. Celsius | Ambient temp. approx. 30 Degree Celsius |
| Dryness | % | 100 |

## 4.3 System Description and Modification

The recent modifications implemented on a 7 MW Captive Power Plant of a major fertiliser industry is evaluated for assessing impact on process system value of the plant on account of modification in Boiler burner management system and De-Super heater in the conversion of a fuel oil fired Boiler to Re Gasified –LNG fired boiler. The power plant consists of three boilers each of capacity 60TPH. Furnace oil is the fuel currently used in the system. For improving energy efficiency the system is modified to dual function mode where the power plant can be operated on Furnace oil as well as on Re-Gasified LNG as per availability of the fuel.

The features of existing arrangement of power plant.

- Three boilers of 60TPH capacity.
- Bidrum arrangement with bank tubes
- Furnace is made of membrane wall arrangement and 3 sets of super heaters viz. LTSH, Platen SH and FSH and economiser is arranged in the intermediate and bank pass of boiler.
- Boiler is provided with front wall firing with FD system and FD fan is supplying required draft.
- Type of air pre heater is tubular air heater type.
- There is a common chimney for all the three boilers.
- Steam Coil Air Pre Heater and Air Pre Heater are provided
- Boiler fitted with 2 burners arranged in one row in the boiler front wall and connected to a common windbox arrangement for the airsupply to the boiler.
- Boiler 1 and 2 – Fire off gas and furnace oil /LSHS
- Boiler 3 – only Furnace oil /LSHS

**Boiler Parameters are**

- Main Steam flow : 60 TPH
- Main Steam pressure : 110 kg /sq.cm
- Main Steam Temp : 520 Deg Celsius
- Boiler Feed water temp : 183 Deg C

## Details of Boiler and burner fittings:

Equipments and Parameters

- No: of boilers - 3 @ 60TPH
- Furnace Width : 4877 mm
- Furnace Depth : 6401 mm
- Draft type : FD

There are two oil burners for each boiler in the situation before modification. The furnace oil and the atomizing steam are fed to the oil gun through the burner.

Refer Fig 3.1 for existing arrangement of burner system and Fig.3.2 for existing lay out of captive power plant.

Refer Fig 3.3 for modified arrangement of Burner System and Ref Fig 3.4 for modified lay out of captive power plant.

The features of existing arrangement of power plant.

- Three boilers of 60TPH capacity.
- Bidrum arrangement with bank tubes
- Furnace is made of membrane wall arrangement and 3 sets of superheaters viz. LTSH,Platen SH and FSH and economiser is arranged in the intermediate and bank pass of boiler.
- Boiler is provided with front wall firing with FD system and FD fan is supplying required draft.
- Type of air pre heater is tubular air heater type.
- There is a common chimney for all the three boilers.
- Steam Coil Air Pre Heater and Air Pre Heater are provided
- Boiler fitted with 2 burners arranged in one row in the boiler front wall and connected to a common windbox arrangement for the airsupply to the boiler.
- Boiler 1 and 2 – Fire off gas and furnace oil /LSHS
- Boiler 3 – only Furnace oil /LSHS

## Boiler Parameters are

- Main Steam flow : 60 TPH
- Main Steam pressure : 110 kg /sq.cm
- Main Steam Temp : 520 Deg Celsius
- Boiler Feed water temp : 183 Deg C

## Details of Boiler and burner fittings:

Equipments and Parameters

- No: of boilers - 3 @ 60TPH
- Furnace Width : 4877 mm
- Furnace Depth : 6401 mm
- Draft type : FD

Refer Table 4.1 for Burner data.

Refer Table 4. 2 for Specification of fuel oil (furnace oil)

Refer Table 4.3 for Specification of off gas

Refer Table 4.4 for Properties of off gas

Refer Table 4.5 for LNG specification

Refer Table 4.6 for Required parameters at Boiler terminal point.

The Captive Power Plant Reliability Data for 8000 hours were taken from the power plant before and after the modification. Collected data MTBF and MTTR before modification are is given in Table 4.7.The Captive power plant components are Feed Water Pump, Steam Header, Steam Turbine, Condenser, Condenser pump, Strainer, Fuel Pump, Heat Exchanger, Air pre heater, Forced Draught Fan, Steam Coil Air Pre Heater, De-Super heater, Platen Super heater, Low Temperature Super Heater, Final Super Heater, Economizer, Start up boiler and LPG- Furnace Oil -Atomizer Steam burner system. After implementation, improvement in MBTF and MTTR are observed in Boiler, and Piping and new values are accounted for LNG Burner System as given in Table 4.8.

### *Table 4. 7: CPP Components MTBF and MTTR Data before Modification*

| Sl no. | CPP components | MTBF (hrs) | MTTR (hrs) |
|---|---|---|---|
| 1 | FWP1 | 7500 | 4 |
| 2 | FWP2 | 7000 | 4 |
| 3 | FWP3 | 7800 | 4 |
| 4 | Boiler | 3000 | 8 |
| 5 | Steam header | 4400 | 3 |
| 6 | Steam turbine | 4400 | 48 |
| 7 | Condenser | 5000 | 8 |
| 8 | Cond. Pump 1 | 3000 | 4 |
| 9 | Cond. Pump 2 | 3000 | 4 |
| 10 | Strainer 1 | 2000 | 3 |
| 11 | Strainer 2 | 2000 | 3 |
| 12 | Strainer 3 | 2000 | 3 |
| 13 | Fuel pump 1 | 4000 | 4 |
| 14 | Fuel pump 2 | 4000 | 4 |
| 15 | Fuel pump 3 | 4000 | 4 |
| 16 | Fuel pump 4 | 4000 | 4 |
| 17 | Fuel pump 5 | 4000 | 4 |
| 18 | Fuel pump 6 | 4000 | 4 |
| 19 | Heat exchanger | 3000 | 8 |
| 20 | FD fan | 4400 | 16 |
| 21 | SCAPH | 3000 | 14 |

| 22 | APH | 3000 | 14 |
| 23 | FSH | 5000 | 48 |
| 24 | DSH | 5500 | 48 |
| 25 | PSH | 8500 | 48 |
| 26 | LTSH | 6000 | 48 |
| 27 | Economiser | 5000 | 48 |
| 28 | Start up boiler | 4000 | 24 |
| 29 | LPG-FO-Atm. Steam Burner System | 3000 | 6 |
| 30 | Chilled water system | 3700 | 5 |
| 31 | Piping | 5000 | 4 |

Refer Table 4.8 for the improved reliability data after modification for the CPP components. Those components are Boiler, LNG Burner system and Piping.

### Table 4.8: CPP components with improved reliability data after modification

| Sl, No. | CPP components | MTBF (hrs) | MTTR (hrs) |
| --- | --- | --- | --- |
| 1 | Boiler | 5000 | 8 |
| 2 | LNG burner system | 7000 | 3 |
| 3 | Piping | 7000 | 4 |

## 4.4 Model Development

The model is developed through a transition of actual configuration into Reliabillity Block

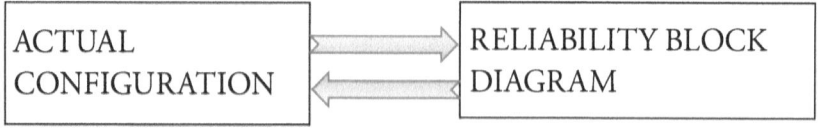

Diagrams. The existing burner arrangement is shown in Fig -3.1 where as burner arrangement after modification is shown in Fig -3.3. The actual configuration before modification is given Fig 3.2. The actual configuration after modification is given in Fig 3.4. The reliability block diagrams are built and shown in Fig 3.8 and Fig 3.9 for before and after modification status respectively.

## 4.5 Existing System of Flame Burner & De-Super heater of Boiler

The existing arrangement of burner have lines of furnace oil supply, 14 Kg/Sq. cm steam,Purge Gas and LPG. Furnace oil supply the main heat energy input to the boiler where as the use of purge gas is as a process bye product utilization. Ref Fig 3.1 for existing arrangement of Burner system.LPG supply is for ignition of burner and ignition is sparked by an electic ignitor. For full load conditions,ie for a steam production rate of 60 TPH, the furnace oil supply rate is 4185 kg/hr. The thermal efficiency of boiler is found to be 67.58 %.The cost of furnace oil is INR 32,000 per Metric Tonne. The furnace oil is used in running the captive power plant of the industry where as the main objective of the plant is steam generation for the production of ammonia which is used for manufacturing fertilizer-

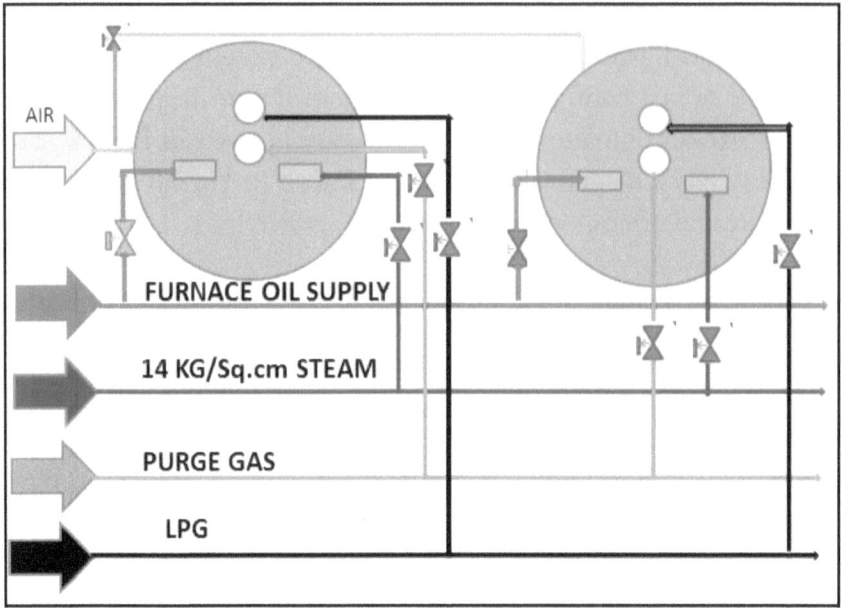

**AIR**

**FURNACE OIL SUPPLY**

**14 KG/Sq.cm STEAM**

**PURGE GAS**

**LPG**

*Fig 4.1 : Existing Arrangement of Burner System*

the prime product of the industry. The power output from the Captive power plant is 7MW electric power. The raw material for manufacturing Ammonia is mainly Naphta which is a bye product after dry distillation of petroleum products. The scope of modification in the power plant is for LNG conversion of the plant on account of the substitution of Naphta with cheaply available(at project initiation phase time period) Regasified LNG. The cost of RLNG at the project initiation time is USD 14.5 per mmBTU.The proposed plan to use RLNG for production of ammonia has resulted in the decision to use the RLNG in captive power plant replacing furnace oil.

There are several advantages on account of LNG Conversion.

1. LNG is cheaply available than furnace oil and hence the fuel cost is low (however scenario changed in due course of time and the condition is dealt in later Section).
2. The heating value of LNG is more than the furnace oil.
3. Boiler maintenance due to of carbon deposit in oil gun, soot formation etc. is eliminated.

4. The requirement of a small capacity start up boiler can be eliminated where the steam from the start up boiler was used to pre- heat the fuel oil and also to generate the atomizing steam.

5. Atomising steam at 7 kg/cm$^2$ is used to atomise furnace oil at the oil gun point to facilitate the smooth firing.

6. Operational and maintenance cost is low due to reduced pipe line accessories and elimination of startup boiler.

7. The reliability and availability of the captive power plant increases

The existing outer dimension of De-Super heater is 1inch and the existing material grade is of low grade as it is causing De –Super heat pipe sagging.

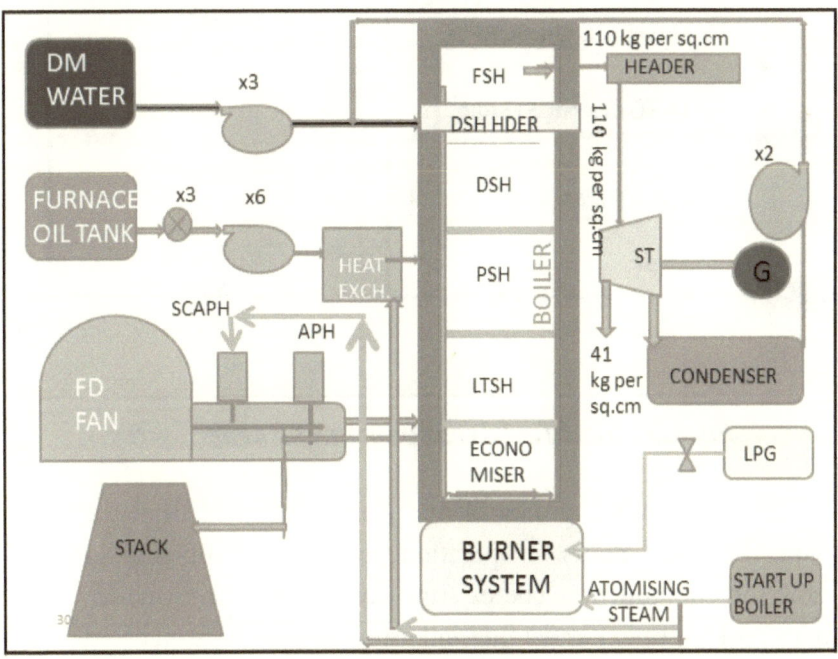

*Fig 4.2 : Existing Layout of Captive Power Plant*

## 4.6 Modified System of Flame Burner
## & De-Super heater of Boiler

The modified arrangement of burner have lines of furnace oil supply, 14 Kg/Sq. cm steam, Purge Gas, LPG and LNG. The new arrangement has a dual function mode. When supply of LNG is not available the plant can be run with furnace oil.

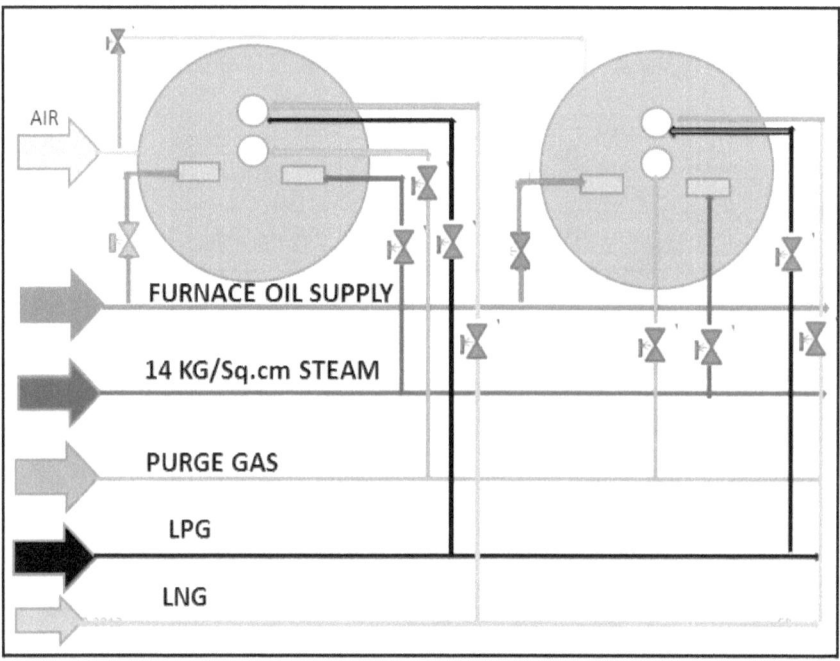

*Fig 4.3 : Modified Arrangement of Burner System*

The plant running data of one year is collected from the power plant. The total hours of operation per year is 8000 hrs. Table 4.7 show the components. The existing lay out is with a smaller header diameter De-Super Header line and using only Furnace oil based burner management system. The modified layout of captive power plant have increased diameter of De-Super Heater pipe and modified flame burner system with additional LNG line. The output parameters of the power plant is not changing due to the modification. The rated power of CPP 7MW, the steam load 60 TPH, Pressure 110 bar and Temperature 520

Deg. Celsius are the same after and before modification. The LNG conversion modification is expected to yield production of more steam at high pressure, hence the De-Super heater diameter increased from 1 inch to 2 inches in order to maintain the initial thermodynamic state parameters. The material grade of De-Super heater pipeline is upgraded to overcome sagging. There are about 31 power plant components/sub systems identified and their MTBF and MTTR are collected from the power plant. The reliability and availability are calculated for these thirty one components /subsystems. There are three subsystems that undergo a change in reliability and availability values due to the modification. They are boiler and piping and burner system. LNG Burner system is a new addition hence its fresh reliability and availability values are calculated.

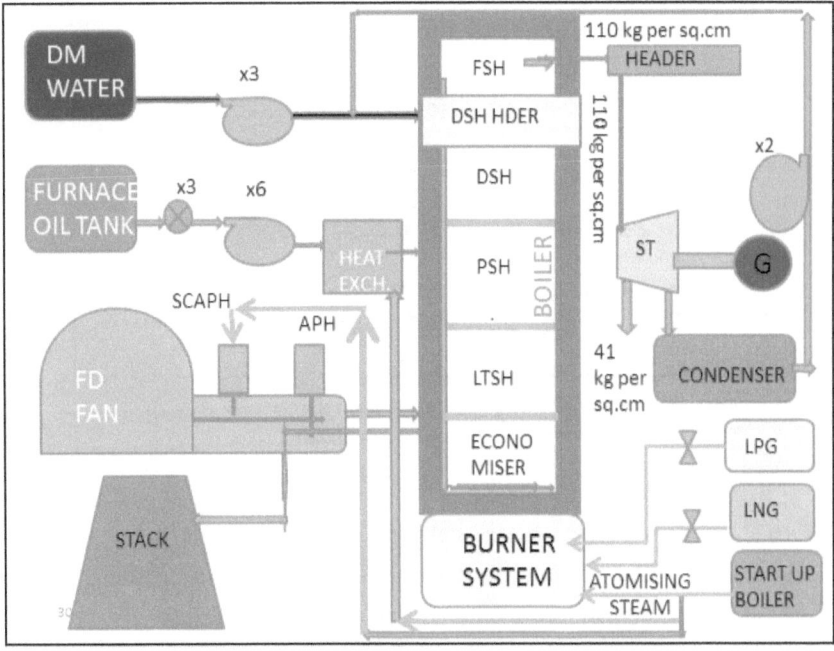

*Fig 4.4 : Modified Layout of Captive Power Plant*

## 4.7 Calculation of System Reliability and Availability

## 4.8 Reliability Block Diagrams

There are three arrangements of reliability block diagrams.

1. Series Arrangement
2. Parallel Arrangement
3. Hybrid arrangement

In Series Arrangement Reliability Block Diagrams are connected in series. Shown in figure 4.5 is a simple series arrangement of three components each having a reliability of 0.90 Then System reliability R $_{s(t)}$ = R$_{1(t)}$ x R$_{2(t)}$ x R$_{3(t)}$

Where R$_{s(t)}$ = System Reliability for given time "t ".

R$_{1....n(t)}$ = Reliability of subsystem components from 1…n for given time (t)

Ref Fig -4.5 for Series arrangement Block diagram.

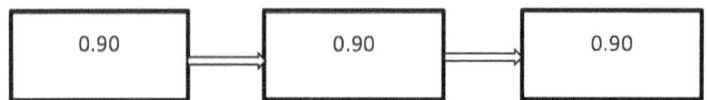

*Fig 4.5 : Reliability Systems in Series Arrangement*

Thus System Reliability R$_{s(t)}$ = 0.9 x 0.9 x 0.9 = 0.729
In Parallel Arrangement Reliability Block Diagrams are connected in parallel to each other. Shown in figure 4.6 is a simple parallel arrangement of three components each having a reliability of 0.90. Then System reliability R $_{s(t)}$ = 1- [(1-R$_{1(t)}$) x (1-R$_{2(t)}$) x (1-R$_{3(t)}$)]

R$_{s(t)}$ = 1- [(1-0.9) x (1-0.9) x (1-0.9)]
= 1-[0.1 x 0.1 x 0.1]
= 0.999

Refer Fig. 4.6 for Parallel arrangement of block diagrams.

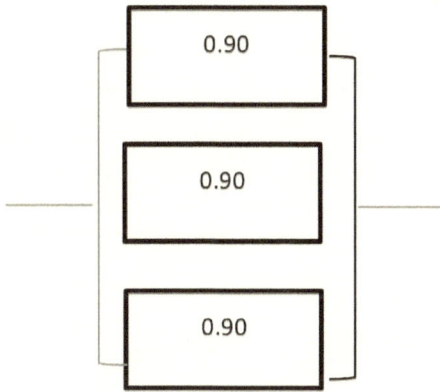

***Fig 4.6: Reliability Systems in Parallel Arrangement***

In hybrid arrangement, the RBD has both series and parallel arrangements of block diagrams. While calculating the system reliability and availability of such arrangements it is necessary to calculate reliability and availability of parallel arrangement first and then connect the entity with series blocks such that final calculation will be that of combined and simplified series arrangement. Refer Fig 4.7.

a)Reliability of parallel arrangement

$$R_{s(t)} = 1- [(1-0.9) \times (1-0.9_) \times (1-0.9)]$$
$$= 1-[0.1 \times 0.1 \times 0.1]$$
$$= 0.999$$

b) System Reliability of Hybrid Arrangement = 0.9 x 0.9 x 0.9 x 0.999
=0.72171

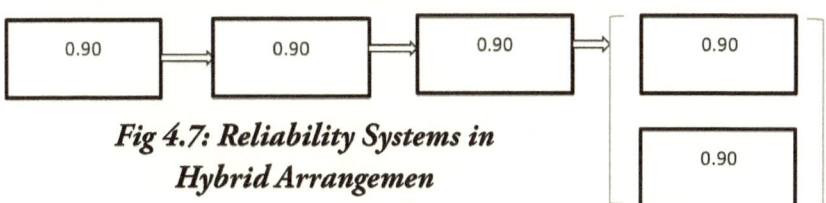

***Fig 4.7: Reliability Systems in***
***Hybrid Arrangemen***

## 4.9 Calculation of System Reliability and Availability before modification

There are 31 individual subsystems/components identified as power plant components for analysis. The reliability and availability of those components are calculated individually. The calculated values are given in Table – 4. 9. The system reliability and availability are evaluated, and the obtained values are

System reliability before modification = 0.0027
System availability before modification =0.9085

Refer Fig -4.8 for the Reliability Block Diagram (RBD) before modification

*Table 4. 9: Reliability and availability before modification*

| Sl No. | CPP COMPONENTS | MTBF (HRS) | MTTR (Hrs) | Availability | Failure rate($\lambda$) | $\lambda *t$ | Reliability =1/(e ^$\lambda *t$) |
|---|---|---|---|---|---|---|---|
| 1 | FWP1 | 7500 | 4 | 0.9995 | 0.00013333 | 0.096 | 0.9085 |
| 2 | FWP2 | 7000 | 4 | 0.9994 | 0.00014286 | 0.10285714 | 0.9023 |
| 3 | FWP3 | 7800 | 4 | 0.9995 | 0.00012821 | 0.09230769 | 0.9118 |
| 4 | BOILER | 3000 | 8 | 0.9997 | 0.00033333 | 0.24 | 0.7866 |
| 5 | STEAM HEADER | 4400 | 3 | 0.9993 | 0.00022727 | 0.16363636 | 0.8491 |
| 6 | STEAM TURBINE | 4400 | 48 | 0.9892 | 0.00022727 | 0.16363636 | 0.8491 |
| 7 | CONDENSER | 5000 | 8 | 0.9984 | 0.0002 | 0.144 | 0.8659 |
| 8 | COND. PUMP 1 | 3000 | 4 | 0.9987 | 0.00033333 | 0.24 | 0.7866 |
| 9 | COND. PUMP 2 | 3000 | 4 | 0.9987 | 0.00033333 | 0.24 | 0.7866 |
| 10 | STRAINER 1 | 2000 | 3 | 0.9985 | 0.0005 | 0.36 | 0.6977 |

| 11 | STRAINER 2 | 2000 | 3 | 0.9985 | 0.0005 | 0.36 | 0.6977 |
| 12 | STRAINER 3 | 2000 | 3 | 0.9985 | 0.0005 | 0.36 | 0.6977 |
| 13 | FUEL PUMP 1 | 4000 | 4 | 0.9990 | 0.00025 | 0.18 | 0.8353 |
| 14 | FUEL PUMP 2 | 4000 | 4 | 0.9990 | 0.00025 | 0.18 | 0.8353 |
| 15 | FUEL PUMP 3 | 4000 | 4 | 0.9990 | 0.00025 | 0.18 | 0.8353 |
| 16 | FUEL PUMP 4 | 4000 | 4 | 0.9990 | 0.00025 | 0.18 | 0.8353 |
| 17 | FUEL PUMP 5 | 4000 | 4 | 0.9990 | 0.00025 | 0.18 | 0.8353 |
| 18 | FUEL PUMP 6 | 4000 | 4 | 0.9990 | 0.00025 | 0.18 | 0.8353 |
| 19 | HEAT EXCHANGER | 3000 | 8 | 0.9973 | 0.00033333 | 0.24 | 0.7866 |
| 20 | FD FAN | 4400 | 16 | 0.9964 | 0.00022727 | 0.16363636 | 0.8491 |
| 21 | SCAPH | 3000 | 14 | 0.9954 | 0.00033333 | 0.24 | 0.7866 |
| 22 | APH | 3000 | 14 | 0.9954 | 0.00033333 | 0.24 | 0.7866 |
| 23 | FSH | 5000 | 48 | 0.9905 | 0.0002 | 0.144 | 0.8659 |
| 24 | DSH | 5500 | 48 | 0.9913 | 0.00018182 | 0.13090909 | 0.8773 |
| 25 | PSH | 8500 | 48 | 0.9944 | 0.00011765 | 0.08470588 | 0.9188 |
| 26 | LTSH | 6000 | 48 | 0.9921 | 0.00016667 | 0.12 | 0.8869 |
| 27 | ECONOMISER | 5000 | 48 | 0.9905 | 0.0002 | 0.144 | 0.8659 |
| 28 | START UP BOILER | 4000 | 24 | 0.9940 | 0.00025 | 0.18 | 0.8353 |
| 29 | LPG-FO-ATM STEAM BURNER SYSTEM | 3000 | 6 | 0.9980 | 0.00033333 | 0.24 | 0.7866 |
| 30 | CHILLED WATER SYSTEM | 3700 | 5 | 0.9980 | 0.00027027 | 0.19459459 | 0.8232 |
| 31 | PIPING | 5000 | 4 | 0.9992 | 0.0002 | 0.144 | 0.8659 |

The CPP components in the reliability block diagram are Feed water pumps,Boiler,Steam header, Steam turbine, Condenser, Condenser pumps,De-aerator, Strainers, Fuel pumps, Heat exchanger, Forced Draught Fan, Steam coil Air pre heater (SCAPH), Air pre heater, De-Super heater, Final Super heater, Platen super heater, Low temperature super heater, Start up boiler, Economizer, LPG-Furnace oil burner, Atomizer, Valve system and Piping.

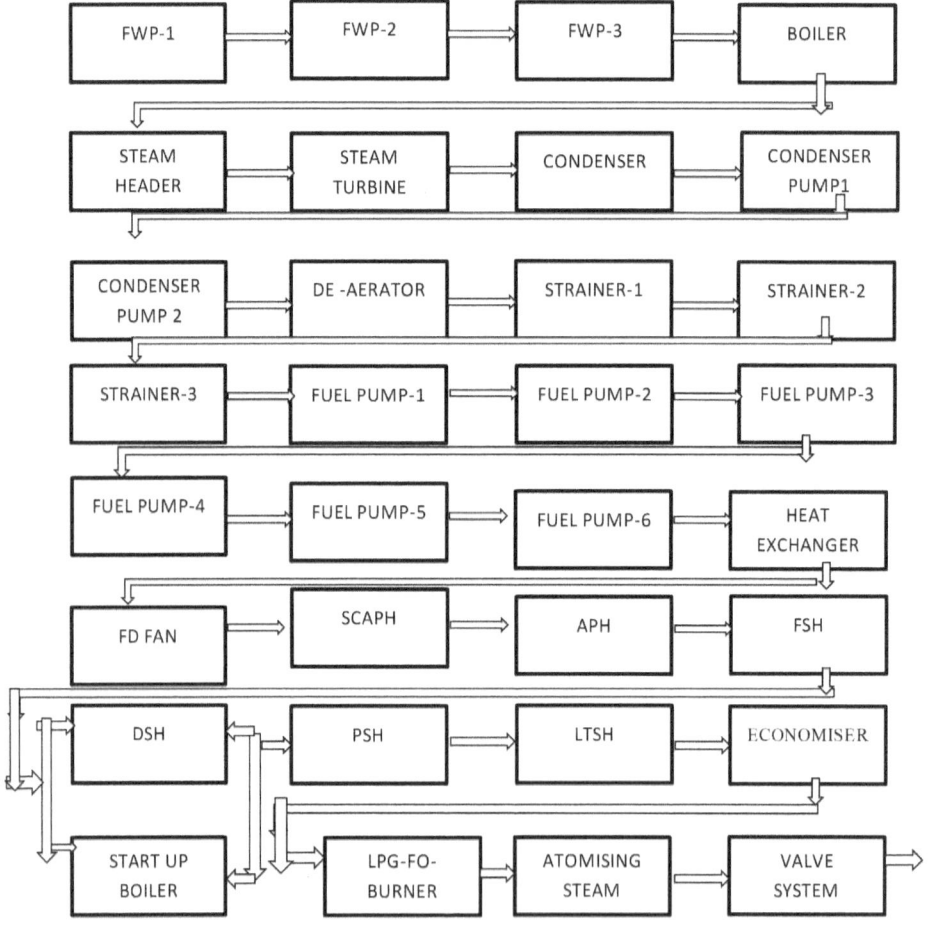

*Fig 4.8: Reliqbility Block Diqgrqm before Modification*

## 4.10 Calculation of System Reliability and Availability after modification

There are 3 individual subsystems/ components that have got an impact on reliability/availability on account of the modification. They are boiler, piping and LNG burner system identified with improved reliability. The newly introduced LNG burner system is added in parallel to the existing LPG Burner system.

The obtained values are given in Table – 4.10. The system reliability and availability after modification are evaluated and the obtained values are

System reliability after modification = 0.003789
System availability after modification =0.9243

Ref Fig 4.9 for RBD after modification. The modification improves the system in terms of reliability and availability. The percentage improvement in System reliability is 1.85% and percentage improvement in System availability is 39.45 %. For reliability calculation, time period "t" is taken as 720 hours.

*Table 4.10 : Reliability and availability after modification*

| Sl No. | CPP COMPONENTS | MTBF(Hrs) | MTTR(Hrs) |
|--------|----------------|-----------|-----------|
| 1 | BOILER | 5000 | 8 |
| 2 | LNG BURNER SYSTEM | 7000 | 3 |
| 3 | PIPING | 7000 | 4 |

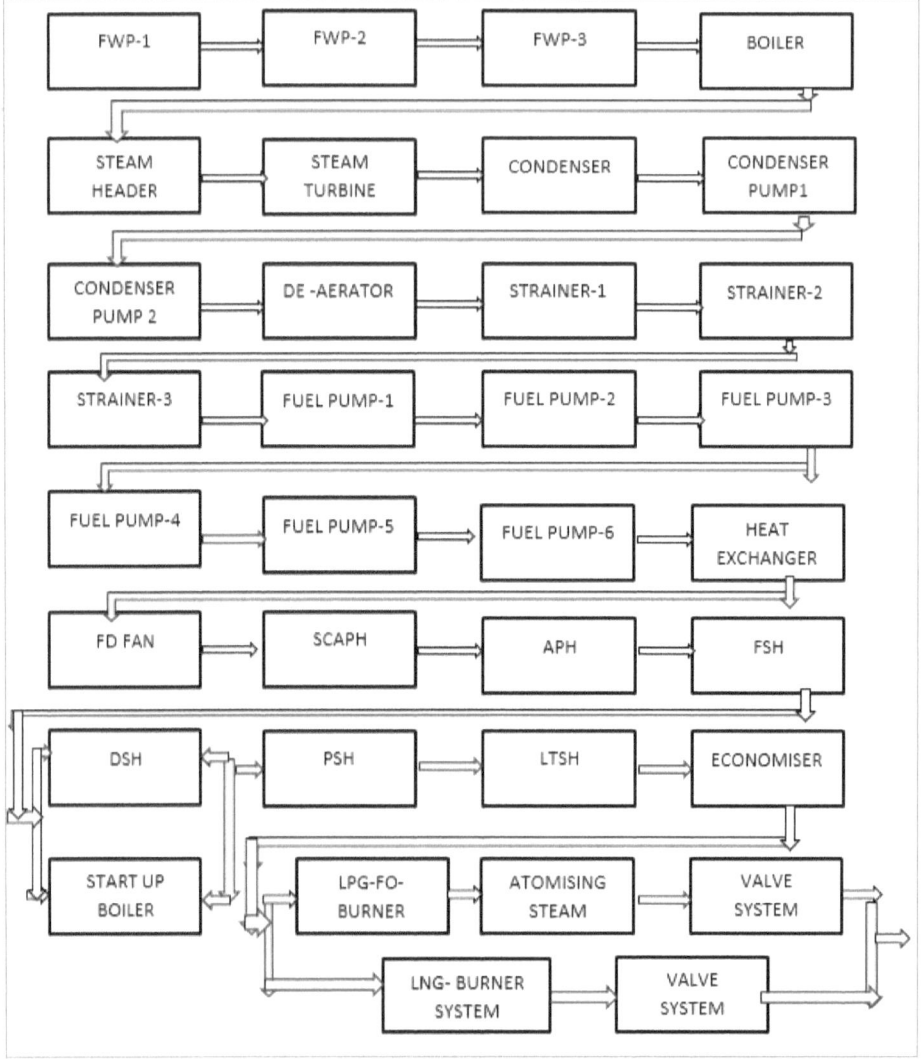

*Fig 4.9 : Reliability Block Diagram after Modification*

## 4.11 Calculation of Process System Value and Pay back period

The data for Process System Value calculation is given in Table 4.11.

The value is calculated using Eqn (10) given in Section 2.

$$V_C = [A_M (RHU - O_M) - A_S (RHU - O_S)] (P/A, i, n) - C_m$$

The system availability before modification is 0.9045 and system availability after modification is 0.9243.

$$V_C = [0.9243((60*8000*2100)-161000000) - 0.9085(60*8000*2100)-182000000](0.9823)-60000000 = INR\ 2.7\ x\ 10^8$$

### Table 4.11: Data for Vc Calculation in Case 1 (When LNG Price is 24.75 USD per MMBTU)

| | |
|---|---|
| System Availability after modification, $A_M$ | 0.9243 |
| System Availability before modification, $A_S$ | 0.9085 |
| Production rate IN Tonneper hour, R | 60 |
| Hours of Operartion per Year, H | 8000 |
| Price per unit process output in INR, U | 2100 |
| Operational and Maintenance Cost after modification, $O_M$ | 161000000 |
| Operational and Maintenance Cost before modification, $O_S$ | 182000000 |
| Rate of Interest, i | 9% |
| Life Expectancy in Years, n | 25 |
| Cost of Modification in INR, $C_m$ | 60000000 |
| ProcessSystemValuein INR, $V_C$ | $2.7\ X10^8$ [Positive] |

The total hours of operation per year, H is 8000 hours. The hourly production rate, R is 60 TPH. The price per unit process output, U is INR 2100. The rate of interest i = 9% and the cost of modification C = INR 60000000. The operational and maintenance cost per year after modification is INR 161000000 where as operational and maintenance cost per year before modification is INR 182000000. With the available data the calculated change in process system value due to modification is found to be INR 2.7 x 10^8

The obtained value of Change in process system value is positive, hence reliability allocation process is not required. The positive value of process system value indicate that the modification cost is recoverable and the investment will earn profit. The total cost of modification is INR 6 0000000. The expected annual savings is INR 2100000 per year. The life expectancy of the captive power plant is considered 25 years.

Simple Pay Back Period can be evaluated as the ratio between Total cost of modification to Expected annual savings

i. e. Simple Pay Back Period = $\dfrac{60000000}{21000000}$ = 2.98 Years

The process evaluation model enable us to accurately determine the payback period from the plot between Life expectancy in Years and Process System Value in each year. The value obtained from the plot is different from the simple pay back period. The accurate pay back period incorporating reliability and availability is found to be 2.4 years. Ref Fig 4.10. The data for plotting fig 4.10 is given in Table 4.12

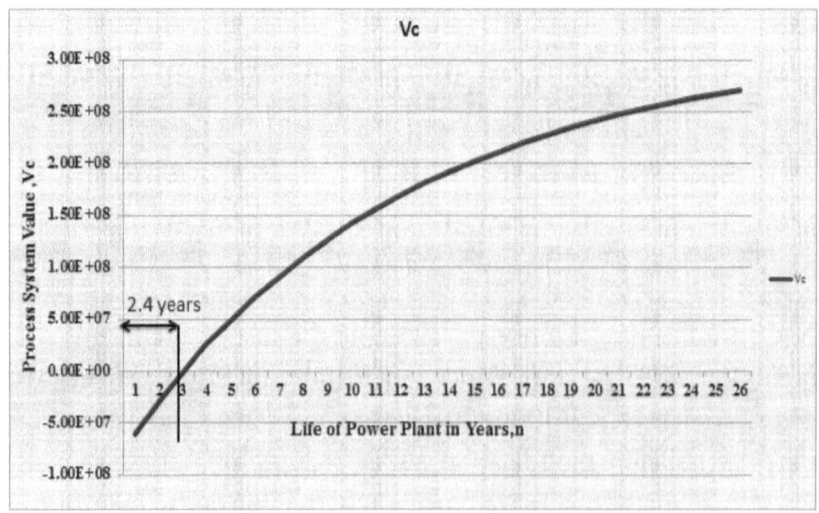

*Fig 4.10: Plot of Process System Value, Vc vs Life of Power Plant in Years, n(Aug 2013)*

The payback period from the plot is less than the simple pay back because the availability of the power plant after modification is more than the availability of the power plant after modification.

**Table 4.12: Data for plot (Fig 4.10) between Process System Value, "Vc" vs Life of Power Plant in Years, "n"**

| n | _Am_ | _As_ | R | H | U | Om | Os | P/A,i,n | Cm | Vc |
|---|------|------|----|------|------|---------|---------|----------|---------|----------|
| 0 | | | | | | | | | | -6.00E+07 |
| 1 | 0.9243 | 0.9085 | 60 | 8640 | 2100 | 1.61E+08 | 1.82E+08 | 0.917431 | 6.00E+07 | -2.91E+07 |
| 2 | 0.9243 | 0.9085 | 60 | 8640 | 2100 | 1.61E+08 | 1.82E+08 | 1.759111 | 6.00E+07 | -6.67E+05 |
| 3 | 0.9243 | 0.9085 | 60 | 8640 | 2100 | 1.61E+08 | 1.82E+08 | 2.531295 | 6.00E+07 | 2.54E+07 |
| 4 | 0.9243 | 0.9085 | 60 | 8640 | 2100 | 1.61E+08 | 1.82E+08 | 3.23972 | 6.00E+07 | 4.93E+07 |
| 5 | 0.9243 | 0.9085 | 60 | 8640 | 2100 | 1.61E+08 | 1.82E+08 | 3.889651 | 6.00E+07 | 7.12E+07 |
| 6 | 0.9243 | 0.9085 | 60 | 8640 | 2100 | 1.61E+08 | 1.82E+08 | 4.485919 | 6.00E+07 | 9.13E+07 |
| 7 | 0.9243 | 0.9085 | 60 | 8640 | 2100 | 1.61E+08 | 1.82E+08 | 5.032953 | 6.00E+07 | 1.10E+08 |
| 8 | 0.9243 | 0.9085 | 60 | 8640 | 2100 | 1.61E+08 | 1.82E+08 | 5.534819 | 6.00E+07 | 1.27E+08 |
| 9 | 0.9243 | 0.9085 | 60 | 8640 | 2100 | 1.61E+08 | 1.82E+08 | 5.995247 | 6.00E+07 | 1.42E+08 |
| 10 | 0.9243 | 0.9085 | 60 | 8640 | 2100 | 1.61E+08 | 1.82E+08 | 6.417658 | 6.00E+07 | 1.56E+08 |
| 11 | 0.9243 | 0.9085 | 60 | 8640 | 2100 | 1.61E+08 | 1.82E+08 | 6.805191 | 6.00E+07 | 1.70E+08 |
| 12 | 0.9243 | 0.9085 | 60 | 8640 | 2100 | 1.61E+08 | 1.82E+08 | 7.160725 | 6.00E+07 | 1.82E+08 |
| 13 | 0.9243 | 0.9085 | 60 | 8640 | 2100 | 1.61E+08 | 1.82E+08 | 7.486904 | 6.00E+07 | 1.93E+08 |
| 14 | 0.9243 | 0.9085 | 60 | 8640 | 2100 | 1.61E+08 | 1.82E+08 | 7.78615 | 6.00E+07 | 2.03E+08 |
| 15 | 0.9243 | 0.9085 | 60 | 8640 | 2100 | 1.61E+08 | 1.82E+08 | 8.060688 | 6.00E+07 | 2.12E+08 |
| 16 | 0.9243 | 0.9085 | 60 | 8640 | 2100 | 1.61E+08 | 1.82E+08 | 8.312558 | 6.00E+07 | 2.20E+08 |
| 17 | 0.9243 | 0.9085 | 60 | 8640 | 2100 | 1.61E+08 | 1.82E+08 | 8.543631 | 6.00E+07 | 2.28E+08 |
| 18 | 0.9243 | 0.9085 | 60 | 8640 | 2100 | 1.61E+08 | 1.82E+08 | 8.755625 | 6.00E+07 | 2.35E+08 |
| 19 | 0.9243 | 0.9085 | 60 | 8640 | 2100 | 1.61E+08 | 1.82E+08 | 8.950115 | 6.00E+07 | 2.42E+08 |
| 20 | 0.9243 | 0.9085 | 60 | 8640 | 2100 | 1.61E+08 | 1.82E+08 | 9.128546 | 6.00E+07 | 2.48E+08 |
| 21 | 0.9243 | 0.9085 | 60 | 8640 | 2100 | 1.61E+08 | 1.82E+08 | 9.292244 | 6.00E+07 | 2.53E+08 |
| 22 | 0.9243 | 0.9085 | 60 | 8640 | 2100 | 1.61E+08 | 1.82E+08 | 9.442425 | 6.00E+07 | 2.58E+08 |
| 23 | 0.9243 | 0.9085 | 60 | 8640 | 2100 | 1.61E+08 | 1.82E+08 | 9.580207 | 6.00E+07 | 2.63E+08 |
| 24 | 0.9243 | 0.9085 | 60 | 8640 | 2100 | 1.61E+08 | 1.82E+08 | 9.706612 | 6.00E+07 | 2.67E+08 |
| 25 | 0.9243 | 0.9085 | 60 | 8640 | 2100 | 1.61E+08 | 1.82E+08 | 9.82258 | 6.00E+07 | 2.71E+08 |

## 4.12 Impact of LNG Price Variation on the Process System Value of the modification

The discussion until now was the scenario of the modification implementation at an LNG price of USD 14.5 per MMBTU in the beginning of August 2013.As per the situation in the mentioned time the change in process system value of the modification is positive. The modification cost was recoverable and the project will yield profits. However due to socio- political and economic conditions, the supply price of LNG is raised to 24.75 USD per MMBTU and the price remains the same value of USD 24.75 as on March 2014. The impact of the price variation can be analyzed using the process evaluation model. The increase in price has caused about 45% in operational cost thus the new value of operational and maintenance cost is INR 23,345,000. Refer Table 4.13 for the new set of data for process evaluation model.

### Table 4.13: Data for Vc Calculation in Case 2(When LNG Price is 24.75 USD per MMBTU)

| | |
|---|---|
| System Availability after modification, $A_M$ | 0.9243 |
| System Availability before modification, $A_S$ | 0.9085 |
| Production rate IN Tonneper hour, R | 60 |
| Hours of Operartion per Year, H | 8000 |
| Price per unit process output in INR, U | 2100 |
| Operational and Maintenance Cost after modification,$O_M$ | 233450000 |
| Operational and Maintenance Cost before modification,$O_S$ | 182000000 |
| Rate of Interest,i | 9% |

| Life Expectancy in Years,n | 25 |
|---|---|
| Cost of Modification in INR,$C_m$ | 60000000 |
| Process SystemValuein INR,$V_C$ | - 9.1 x $10^7$ [Negative] |

The value is calculated using Eqn (10) given in Section 2.

$$V_C = [A_M (RHU - O_M) - A_S (RHU - O_S)] (P/A, i,n) - C_m$$

The system availability before modification is 0.9045 and system availability after modification is 0.9243.

$$V_C = [0.9243((60*8000*2100)- 233450000) - 0.9085(60*8000*2100)- 182000000](0.9823)-60000000 = - 9.1 \times 10^7 \text{ [Negative]}$$

Since the change in process system value is negative, the modification cost cannot be recovered and the project will not earn profits due to the socio economic and political situations. When the graph is plotted for n=1 to 25, the line of value $V_c$ is parting away from the X-Axis and is not showing any improvement over the period if the LNG supply price is USD 24.75 mmBTU. Refer Fig 4.11 for plot in Case 2. Data for plot is given in Table 4.14. Refer Fig 4.12 for combined plot between Case 1 and Case 2.

Case 1: LNG price = USD 14.5 per MMBTU
Case 2 : LNG price = USD 24.75 per MMBTU

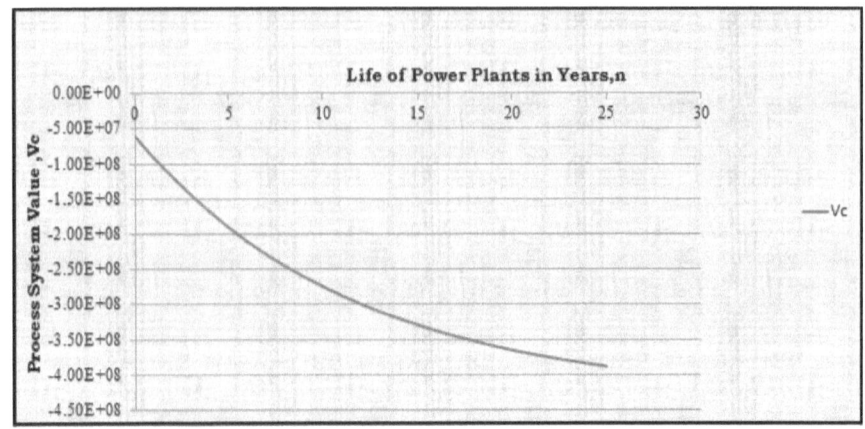

**Fig 4.11: Plot of Process System Value,Vc vs Life of Power Plant in Years,n(April 2014)**

**Table 14: Data for plot(Fig 4.11) between Process System Value, "Vc "vs Life of Power Plant in Years, "n"**

| n | Am | As | R | H | U | Om | Os | P/A,i,n | Cm | Vc |
|---|-----|-----|----|------|------|---------|---------|----------|---------|----------|
| 0 | | | | | | | | | | -6.00E+07 |
| 1 | 0.9243 | 0.9085 | 60 | 8640 | 2100 | 1.61E+08 | | 0.917431 | 6.00E+07 | -9.06E+07 |
| 2 | 0.9243 | 0.9085 | 60 | 8640 | 2100 | 1.61E+08 | 2.34E+08 | 1.759111 | 6.00E+07 | -1.19E+08 |
| 3 | 0.9243 | 0.9085 | 60 | 8640 | 2100 | 1.61E+08 | 2.34E+08 | 2.531295 | 6.00E+07 | -1.45E+08 |
| 4 | 0.9243 | 0.9085 | 60 | 8640 | 2100 | 1.61E+08 | 2.34E+08 | 3.23972 | 6.00E+07 | -1.68E+08 |
| 5 | 0.9243 | 0.9085 | 60 | 8640 | 2100 | 1.61E+08 | 2.34E+08 | 3.889651 | 6.00E+07 | -1.90E+08 |
| 6 | 0.9243 | 0.9085 | 60 | 8640 | 2100 | 1.61E+08 | 2.34E+08 | 4.485919 | 6.00E+07 | -2.10E+08 |
| 7 | 0.9243 | 0.9085 | 60 | 8640 | 2100 | 1.61E+08 | 2.34E+08 | 5.032953 | 6.00E+07 | -2.28E+08 |
| 8 | 0.9243 | 0.9085 | 60 | 8640 | 2100 | 1.61E+08 | 2.34E+08 | 5.534819 | 6.00E+07 | -2.45E+08 |
| 9 | 0.9243 | 0.9085 | 60 | 8640 | 2100 | 1.61E+08 | 2.34E+08 | 5.995247 | 6.00E+07 | -2.60E+08 |
| 10 | 0.9243 | 0.9085 | 60 | 8640 | 2100 | 1.61E+08 | 2.34E+08 | 6.417658 | 6.00E+07 | -2.74E+08 |
| 11 | 0.9243 | 0.9085 | 60 | 8640 | 2100 | 1.61E+08 | 2.34E+08 | 6.805191 | 6.00E+07 | -2.87E+08 |
| 12 | 0.9243 | 0.9085 | 60 | 8640 | 2100 | 1.61E+08 | 2.34E+08 | 7.160725 | 6.00E+07 | -2.99E+08 |
| 13 | 0.9243 | 0.9085 | 60 | 8640 | 2100 | 1.61E+08 | 2.34E+08 | 7.486904 | 6.00E+07 | -3.10E+08 |
| 14 | 0.9243 | 0.9085 | 60 | 8640 | 2100 | 1.61E+08 | 2.34E+08 | 7.78615 | 6.00E+07 | -3.20E+08 |
| 15 | 0.9243 | 0.9085 | 60 | 8640 | 2100 | 1.61E+08 | 2.34E+08 | 8.060688 | 6.00E+07 | -3.29E+08 |
| 16 | 0.9243 | 0.9085 | 60 | 8640 | 2100 | 1.61E+08 | 2.34E+08 | 8.312558 | 6.00E+07 | -3.38E+08 |
| 17 | 0.9243 | 0.9085 | 60 | 8640 | 2100 | 1.61E+08 | 2.34E+08 | 8.543631 | 6.00E+07 | -3.45E+08 |

| 18 | 0.9243 | 0.9085 | 60 | 8640 | 2100 | 1.61E+08 | 2.34E+08 | 8.755625 | 6.00E+07 | -3.52E+08 |
| 19 | 0.9243 | 0.9085 | 60 | 8640 | 2100 | 1.61E+08 | 2.34E+08 | 8.950115 | 6.00E+07 | -3.59E+08 |
| 20 | 0.9243 | 0.9085 | 60 | 8640 | 2100 | 1.61E+08 | 2.34E+08 | 9.128546 | 6.00E+07 | -3.65E+08 |
| 21 | 0.9243 | 0.9085 | 60 | 8640 | 2100 | 1.61E+08 | 2.34E+08 | 9.292244 | 6.00E+07 | -3.70E+08 |
| 22 | 0.9243 | 0.9085 | 60 | 8640 | 2100 | 1.61E+08 | 2.34E+08 | 9.442425 | 6.00E+07 | -3.75E+08 |
| 23 | 0.9243 | 0.9085 | 60 | 8640 | 2100 | 1.61E+08 | 2.34E+08 | 9.580207 | 6.00E+07 | -3.80E+08 |
| 24 | 0.9243 | 0.9085 | 60 | 8640 | 2100 | 1.61E+08 | 2.34E+08 | 9.706612 | 6.00E+07 | -3.84E+08 |
| 25 | 0.9243 | 0.9085 | 60 | 8640 | 2100 | 1.61E+08 | 2.34E+08 | 9.82258 | 6.00E+07 | -3.88E+08 |

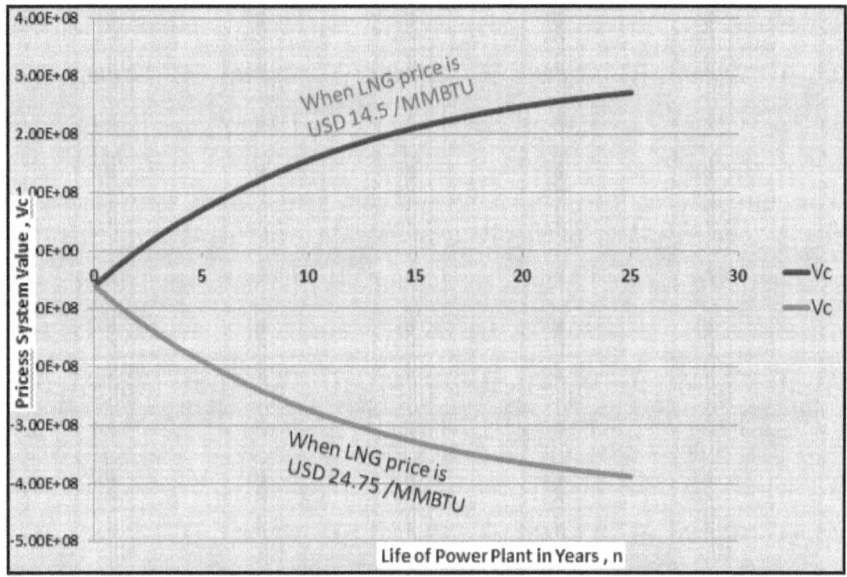

*Fig 4.12: Combined Plot of Process System Value,*
*Vc vs Life of Power Plant in Years,n*

## 4.13 First Law and Second Law Efficiency Analysis of Captive Power Plant Components

This section evaluate the first law and second law efficiency analysis of the major power plant components Boiler and Steam Turbine. The efficiency analysis of Condenser and De-Aerator is also evaluated.

Ref Fig 4.13 for the schematic diagram of the captive power plant incorporating modifications.

The water stored in the De-Mineralised water tank fed to the Boiler by means of centrifugal boiler feed pumps. The boiler feed water has an initial temperature of 138 Deg C and 145 bar pressure. The boiler consists of Economiser, Platen Super Heater, De-Super Heater and Final Super Heater. The steam received in the header after Final Super Heater has Thermodynamic parameters 510 Deg C and 110 bar Pressure. The fuel system before modification has only furnace oil as the fuel where as in the modified system the captive plant functions on dual mode where the fuel system consists of arrangement to feed furnace oil as well as RLNG depending on availability. For the maximum load of boiler, ie The pressure of RLNG is 4 bar at boiler terminal point. For full load capacity,the feed value of furnace oil is 4183 kg/hr for 1 tonne of steam where as in case of RLNG is 62 kg/hr to generate 1 tonne of steam. The combustion air is supplied by forced draft fan per boiler. In case of furnace oil system atomizing steam is supplied along with furnace oil at oil gun. In case of LNG, there is no requirement of atomizing steam.

The furnace oil in the fuel tank is pumped by means of 3 fuel pumps through 6 strainers. The fuel oil is heated by means of heat exchanger where heat transfer take place between steam and oil.

The combustion air is supplied by the Forced Draft Fan,and the air is preheated by two means, one by mechanical air pre heater and other by means of SCAPH (Steam Coil Air Pre Heater).

The steam from the boiler is fed to the turbine inlet where the conditions of steam are at 510 Deg C temp and 110 bar. The turbine has an extraction point at 41 bar pressure and steam from the extraction point is supplied to process plant for manufacturing ammonia. The mass of steam taken from extraction point is 35 TPH and temperature of extracted steam is 300 Deg C. The condensing pressure is vacuum at the turbine outlet. The turbine out let steam conditions are 25 TPH, 65 Deg C and 0.5 bar. The rated power of the Captive Power Plant is 7MW.

The quality of steam entering the condenser has a dryness fraction of 0.95. The mass of cooling water flowing to condenser is 784 TPH. The inlet temperature of cooling water is 35 Deg C where as outlet temperature 52 Deg C. The saturation temperature of condensing steam is 65 Deg C.

The condensate is pumped to the De-Aerator where the circulating water is de-aerated and heated. The de-aerated steam is at 5 bar and the mass flow rate of steam is 5 TPH. The deaerated condensate is pumped to the boiler feed inlet

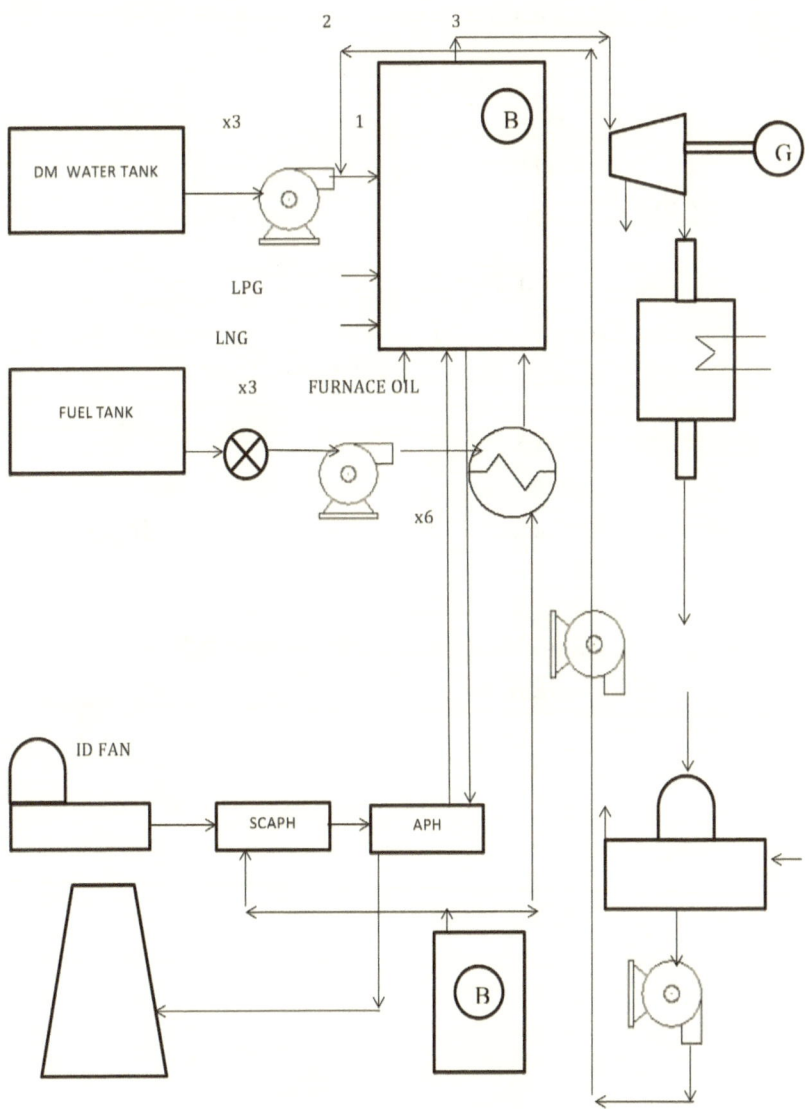

*Fig 4.13 : Schematic of Power Plant*

### 4.13.1 First Law Efficiency of Boiler Before and After Modification:

#### 4.13.1.1 First Law Efficiency of Boiler Before Modification:

Ref Fig 4.14 for Control Volume of Boiler before modification. And Fig 4.15 for Control volume of boiler after modification.

$Q_k$ = Fuel Oil Flow x Heating Value

$$= 4131 \times 9180$$
$$= 37,922,580 \text{ kCal/Hr}$$
$$= 37,922,580 \times 4.183$$
$$\underline{= 158,630,152 \text{ kJ/hr}}$$

- ➤ From Steam Tables, Corresponding to $P_1$, $T_2$, $P_2$
- ➤ Specific Enthalpy, $h_1 @ T_1 = 185$ °C $P_1 = 145$ bar = 782 kJ/kg
- ➤ Specific Enthalpy, $h_2 @ T_2 = 510$ °C; $P_2 = 110$ bar

$$= 3400 \text{ kJ/kg}$$

- ➤ First Law Efficiency = Energy Output / Energy Input

$$= m_w (h_2 - h_1)/Q_k$$
$$= 60000 (3400-782) /158,630,152$$
$$= 98.6 \%$$

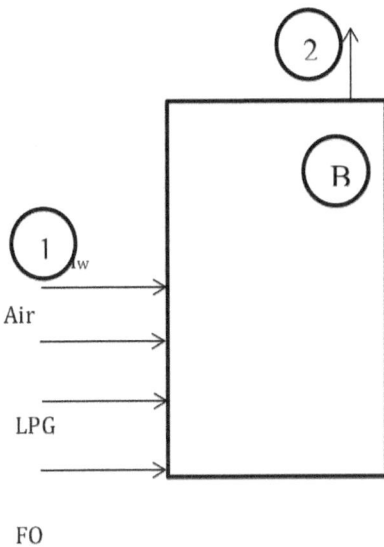

*Fig 4.14: Control Volume of Boiler before modification*

## 4.13.1.2 First Law Efficiency Analysis of Boiler after Modification:

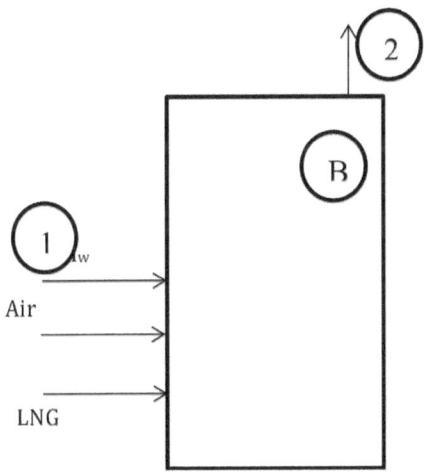

*Fig 4.15: Control Volume of Boiler after modification*

➢ From Steam Tables, Corresponding to $P_1$, $T_2$, $P_2$
➢ Specific Enthalpy, $h_1@T_1$ = 183 Deg C, $P_1$ =145ata = 782 kJ/kg
➢ Specific Enthalpy, $h_2@$ $T_2$ =510 °C; $P_{2=}$ 110 ata = 3400 kJ/kg

➢ 1 ton of Steam require 62.511kg/hr of Regasified LNG@4bar,25 Deg C

Heating Value of RLNG = 10000 kCal/SCM and
Density of RLNG = 0.771 kg/SCM
Heating Value in kJ/kg =(10000/0.771) x 4.183

=54,255 kJ/hr

$Q_k$ = 54,255 kJ/hr x 62.511= 203,489,115 kJ/hr

➢ First Law Efficiency = Energy O/P / Energy Input

$$= m_w \ (h_2 - h_1)/Q_k$$
$$= 60000(3400 - 782) \ /203,489,115$$
$$= 77.1 \ \%$$

## 4.13.2 Second Law Efficiency of Boiler before and after Modification:

### 4.13.2.1 Second Law Efficiency of Boiler Before Modification:

Fuel firing rate = 4131 Kg/ Hr.
$T_0$ = 25 Deg C
Mean Heat Capacity of FO CMHC= 1.657 Kj/Kg Deg K

$$\eta II = \frac{mw \ [(h2-h1)w - T0 \ (s2-s1)w) \ ]}{mf \ [(h2-h1)f - T0 \ (s2-s1)f]}$$

$$\frac{60000 \ [(3400-782) \ -298(6.6-3.655) \ ]}{4131[(9180x4.183 - 1.657x118) - 298x1.657x \ln(451/298)]}$$

= **65.7 %**

### 4.13.2.2 Second Law Efficiency of Boiler After Modification:

Mean Heat Capacity of RLNG = 2.34 kJ/kg K

$$\eta II = \frac{mw\ [(h2-h1)w-T0\ (s2-s1)w)\ ]}{mf\ [(h2-h1)f-T0\ (s2-s1)f]}$$

$$\frac{60000\ [(3400-1582)\ -298(6.6-3.655)\ ]}{3750[(11610x4.183-2.34x118)-298x2.34x\ln(451/298)]}$$

= **58.05 %**

### 4.13.3 First Law Eficiency Analysis of Steam Turbine Before and After Modification:

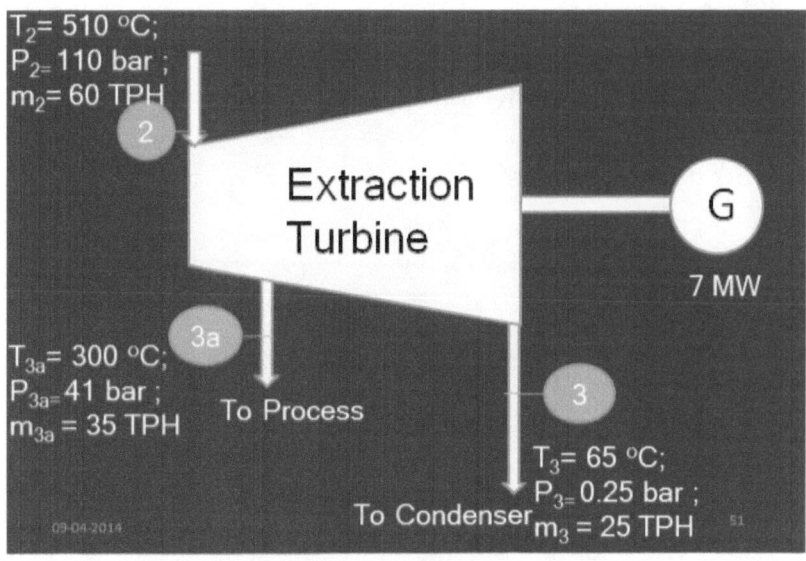

*Fig 4.16: Control Volume of Steam Turbine*
*(Same before and after modification)*

**Assumptions:**
1. **Transmission efficiency as per the manufacturer is 98.40 %**
2. **Generator efficiency as per the manufacturer is 98.03 %**

Refer Fig 4.16 for Control Volume of Steam Turbine*(Same before and after modification)*

Energy input is equal to product of mass of steam into turbine and its enthalpy at entry.

Energy Balance :

$m_2 \times h_2 = m_{3a} \times h_{3a} + m_3 \times h_3 + W_T +$ Energy Losses

$E_I = m_2 \times h_2$

= 60000 kg/hr x 3362 kJ/kg

= 201,720,000 kJ/hr

= *2.01 x 10$^8$ kJ/hr*

Energy at Outlet

$E_O = m_{3a} \times h_{3a} + m_3 \times h_3$

= 35,000 kg/hr x 2962kJ/kg + 25,000 kg/hr x 2618 kJ/kg

= 169,120,000 kJ/hr

= ***1.69x10$^8$ kJ/hr***

Work done by turbine,

$W = E_I - E_O$

= 201,720,000 - 170,995,000

=32,600,000 kJ/hr

= ***3.26 x 10$^6$ kJ/hr***

Rated Power of CPP =7 MW

=7000 kW

=7000 x 60 x 60

= 25,200,000 kJ/hr

Actual Work done by Turbine

$W_T$ = (25,200,000) / (0.98 x 0.98)

= ***26,239,067 kJ/hr***

= ***2.62 x10$^7$ kJ/hr***

First Law Efficiency of Turbine

$= W_{actual} / E_I - E_O$

= 2.62 x 10$^7$ kJ/hr /3.26 x 10$^7$ kJ/hr

= ***80.4 %***

$m_2 \times h_2 = m_{3a} \times h_{3a} + m_3 \times h_3 + W_{actual} +$ Energy Losses

$E_i = E_o + W_T +$ Energy Losses

Energy Losses= $E_i - E_o - W_{actual}$

Energy Losses=***2.01 x 10$^8$ kJ/hr - 1.66 x10$^8$ kJ/hr***

$$- 2.62 \times 10^{7} kJ/hr$$
$$= 9.2 \times 10^{6} kJ/hr$$

There are no change in thermodynamic parameters before and after modification, hence first law efficiency before and after modification are same.

## 4.13.4 Second Law Efficiency Analysis of Steam Turbine Before and After Modification:

Exergy Inlet :
$$\Psi_{in} = \Psi_2 = m_2 [(h_2 - h_0) - T_0(s_2 - s_0)]$$
$$= 60000 \text{ kg/hr} \times [(3362 \text{ kJ/kg} - 105 \text{ kJ/kg})$$
$$- 298 \text{ Deg K } (6.543 - 0.367)]$$
$$= 84{,}993{,}120 \text{ kJ/hr}$$
$$= \mathbf{8.5 \times 10^{7} kJ/hr}$$

$$\Psi_{3a} = m_{3a} [(h_{3a} - h_0) - T_0(s_{3a} - s_0)]$$
$$= 35000 \text{ kg/hr } [(2644 \text{ kJ/kg} - 105 \text{ kJ/kg})$$
$$- 298 \text{ Deg K } \times (7.609 - 0.367)]$$
$$= 13{,}330{,}940 \text{ kJ/hr}$$
$$= \mathbf{1.33 \times 10^{7} kJ/hr}$$

$$\Psi_3 = m_3 [(h_3 - h_0) - T_0(s_3 - s_0)]$$
$$= 25000 \text{ kg/hr } [(2501 \text{ kJ/kg} - 105 \text{ kJ/kg})$$
$$- 298 \text{ Deg K } \times (7.202 - 0.367)]$$
$$= 8{,}979{,}250 \text{ kJ/hr}$$
$$= 8.98 \times 10^{6} kJ/hr$$

$$\Psi_{out} = \Psi_3 + \Psi_{3a}$$
$$= 8{,}979{,}250 \text{ kJ/hr} + 13{,}330{,}940 \text{ kJ/hr}$$
$$= 22{,}310{,}190 \text{ kJ/hr}$$

Exergetic Efficiency(Second Law) Efficiency
$$= \Psi_{turbine \, Power} / (\Psi_{in} - \Psi_{out})$$
$$= 26{,}239{,}067 \text{ kJ/hr} / (84{,}993{,}120 - 22{,}310{,}190)$$
$$= \mathbf{41.8 \%}$$

*Since initial and final thermodynamic parameters do not change due to process system modifications, Second Law Efficiency of Steam Turbine are same before and after modifications.*

### 4.13.5 First Law Efficiency Analysis of Condenser Before and After Modification:

➢ Efficiencies are not readily defined for the condensers, as the purpose of such devices is to reject waste heat rather than generate a product. [Ibrahim Dincer and Mc A Rosen]

➢ However, the merit of the condensers with respect to the overall plant can be assessed for comparative purposes by evaluating the **'net station condenser heat (energy) rejection rate'** $R_{energy}$, and [Ibrahim Dincer and Mc A Rosen] and **'net station condenser exergy rejection rate** $R_{exergy}$

Ref Fig 4.17 for Control Volume of Condenser (Same before and after modification)

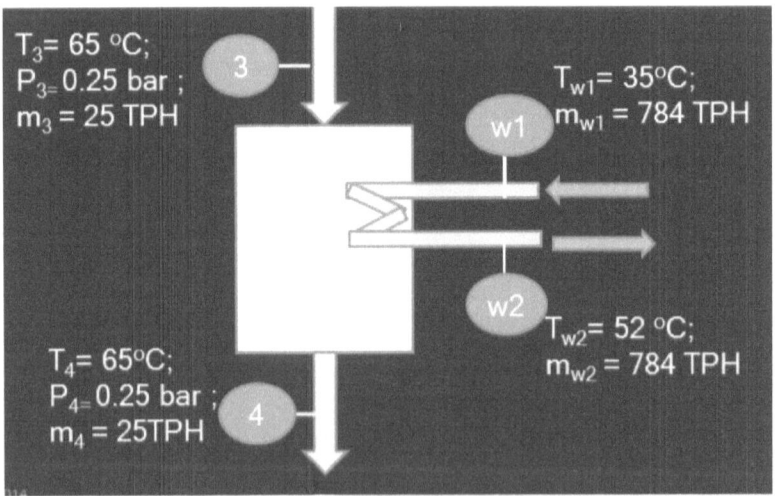

*Fig 4.17: Control Volume of Condenser(Same before and after modification)*

$$FirstLawCondenserEfficiency = \frac{Tw2-Tw1}{Ts-Tw1} = \frac{52-35}{65-35} = 68\%$$

where

*Net station condenser heat (energy) rejection rate*

$$Re\,nergy = \frac{\text{Energy rejected in Condenser}}{\text{Net Electrical Energy Produced}}$$

Quality of Steam Entering Condenser:

Turbine $_{\text{Work Output}}$ = $m_2\, x(h_2-h_{3a}) + m_3\, x(h_{3a}-h_3)$

26,239,067 kJ/hr = 60,000 kg/hr x(3362 − 3215)kJ/kg +25000 kg/hr

x (3215- (272 + c x 2346))kJ/kg

=8820 000 +120575000 − 638112 x c

=26 239 067

Dryness Fraction, c =

(8820 000 +120575000 -26 239 067)/638112

= **0.95**

$m_{cs}x(h_3-h_4) = m_{cw}\, x(h_{w2} - h_{w1})$

25000 kg/hr x ((272 + 0.95 x 2346) - 272)kJ/kg =

$m_{cw}$ kg/hr x(217.6 - 146.6)kJ/kg

$m_{cw}$ = 25000 kg/hr x ((272 + 0.95 x 2346) - 272)kJ/kg /

(217.6 -146.6)kJ/kg

=784,753 kg/hr

= **784 TPH**

Energy Rejected in Condenser = $m_{cs}\,(h_3-h_4)$

=(25000 kg/hr x (272 + 0.95 x 2346 - 272))kJ/kg)

=56,857,500 kJ/hr

Net Electrical Energy Produced = 7 MW

= 25,200,000 kJ/hr

$R_{\text{energy}}$ = 56,857,500 /25,200,000 = **2.25**

> There is no change in inlet and outlet parameters, Pressure, Temperature and Load on account of modification.

> ➢ Hence the first law efficiency before and after modification are the same.

## 4.13.6 Second Law Efficiency Analysis of Condenser Before Modification:

$$\text{Re } xergy = \frac{\text{Exergy rejected in Condenser}}{\text{Net Electrical Exergy Produced}}$$

Exergy Rejected in Condenser
$= m_{cs} [(h_3-h_4)-T_0(s3-s4)]$
$=25000$ kg/hr x $[(272 + 0.95$ x $2346)-272$ kJ/kg$]-$
$\quad 298$ x$[(0.893 +0.95$ x $6.939) -0.893]$
$=6,606,728$ kJ/hr

## 4.13.7 First Law Efficiency Analysis of De Aerator Before and After Modification:

> ➢ *There is no change in inlet and outlet parameters, Pressure, Temperature and Load on account of modification.*
> ➢ *Hence the first law efficiency of De-Aerator before and after modification are the same*
> ➢ *Ref Fig 4.18 for control volume of De-Aerator before and after modification.*

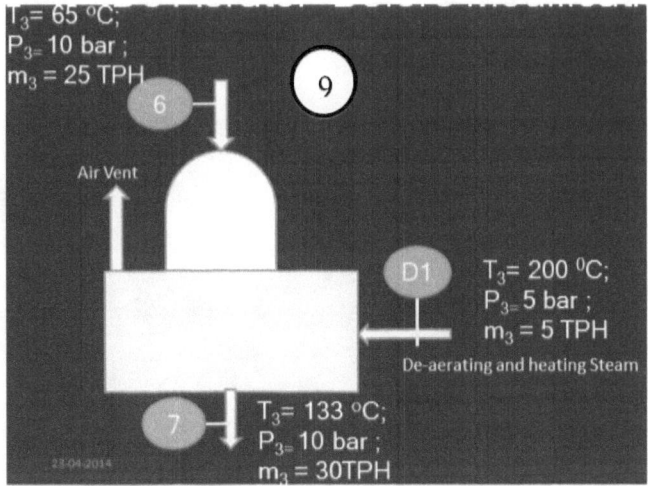

*Fig 4.18: Control Volume of De-Aerator(Same before and after modification)*

First Law Efficiency of De-Aerator

$$= \frac{m7 \times h7}{m6xh6 + mD1xhD1}$$

$$= \frac{30,000x560}{25,000x272 + 5000x2855}$$

$$= 79.7\%$$

## 4.13.8 Second Law Efficiency Analysis of De Aerator Before and After Modification:

Second Law Efficiency of De - Aerator

$$= \frac{m7 \times [(h7 - h0) - T0(s7 - s0)]}{m6x[(h6 - h0) - T0(s6 - s0) + mD1x[(hD1 - h0) - T0(sD1 - s0)]}$$

$$= \frac{30,000x[(560-108) - 298(1.660 - 0.367)]}{25,000x[(272-108) - 298(0.893 - 0.367)] + 5000x[(2747.5 - 108) - 298(7.059 - 0.367)]}$$

$$= \frac{2,000,580}{181300 + 3,226,420}$$

$$= 58.7\%$$

➢ **There is no change in inlet and outlet parameters, Pressure, Temperature and Load on account of modification.**

➤ Hence the first law efficiency before and after modification are the same.

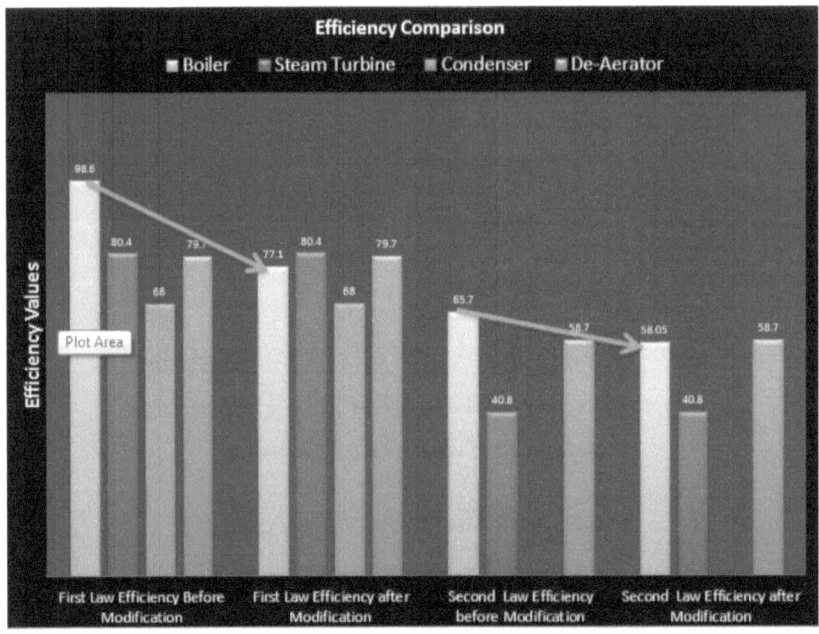

*Fig 4.19: Efficiency Comparison Bar Chart*

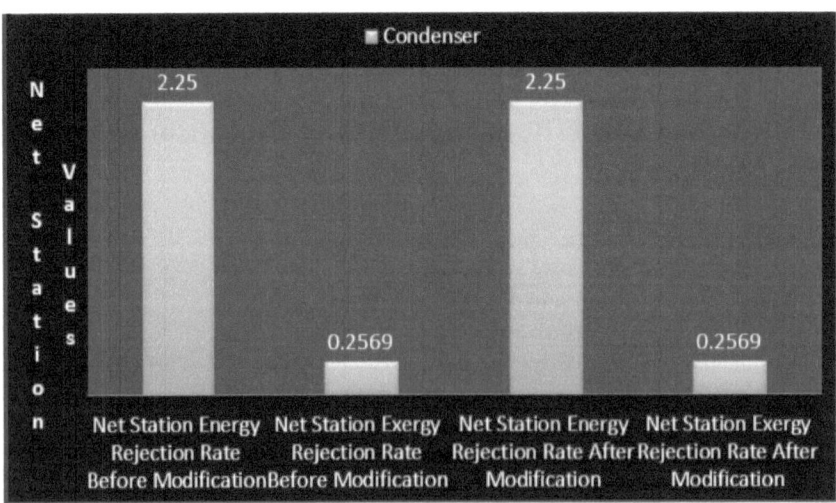

*Fig 4.20: Net Station Energy/Exergy Rejection Rates Comparison-Condenser*

## 4.14 Correlation between Availability and Second Law Efficiency

The table below shows the reliability and availability of those components whose second law efficiency are evaluated before and after modification.

### Table 4.13: Reliability Data of Efficiency Evaluated components before Modification

| Sl.No. | CPP COMPONENTS | MTBF( HRS) | MTTR( Hrs) | Availability | Failure rate(λ) | λ *t | Reliabilit y =1/(e ^λ *t) |
|--------|----------------|------------|------------|--------------|------------------|------|---------------------------|
| 1 | BOILER | 3000 | 8 | 0.9997 | 0.00033 333 | 0.24 | 0.7866 |
| 2 | STEAM TURBINE | 4400 | 48 | 0.9892 | 0.00022 727 | 0.1636363 6 | 0.8491 |
| 3 | CONDENSER | 5000 | 8 | 0.9984 | 0.0002 | 0.144 | 0.8659 |
| 4 | DE-AERATOR | 3000 | 4 | 0.9987 | 0.00033 333 | 0.24 | 0.7866 |

### Table 4.14: Reliability Data of Efficiency Evaluated components after Modification

| Sl.No. | CPP COMPONENTS | MTBF( HRS) | MTTR( Hrs) | Availability | Failure rate(λ) | λ *t | Reliabilit y =1/(e ^λ *t) |
|--------|----------------|------------|------------|--------------|------------------|------|---------------------------|
| 1 | BOILER | 5000 | 8 | 0.9998 | 0.0002 | 0.144 | 0.8869 |
| 2 | STEAM TURBINE | 4400 | 48 | 0.9892 | 0.00022 727 | 0.1636363 6 | 0.8491 |
| 3 | CONDENSER | 5000 | 8 | 0.9984 | 0.0002 | 0.144 | 0.8659 |
| 4 | DE-AERATOR | 3000 | 4 | 0.9987 | 0.00033 333 | 0.24 | 0.7866 |

There are 4 components Boiler, Steam Turbine, Condenser and De-Aerator whose Second Law Efficiency are evaluated.The availability values are 0.9997, 0.9892, 0.9984 and 0.9987 respectively before modification and 0.9998, 0.9892, 0.9984 and 0.9987 respectively after modification. Due to modification, the component among the 4 where reliability and availability is improved is Boiler.

Ref Fig 4.21 and 4.22 for analysis of comparison.

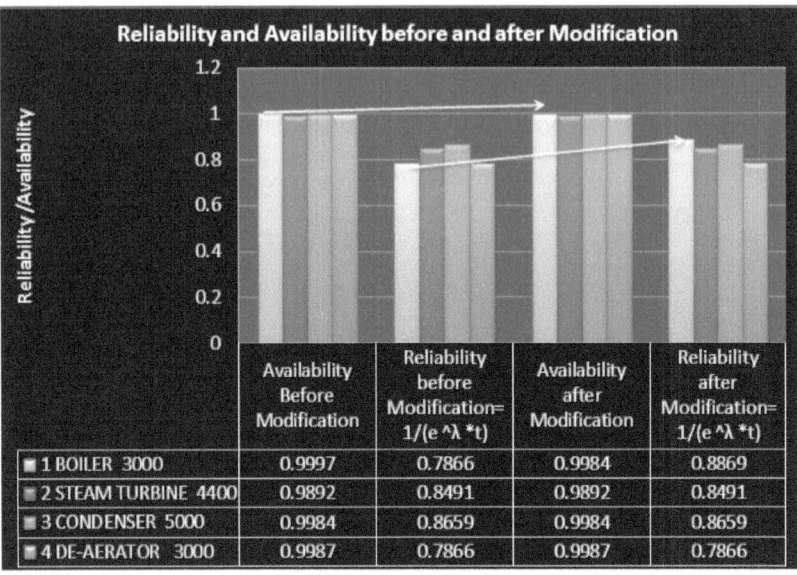

*Fig 4.21: Correlation Chart for Availability –
Second Law Efficiency Comparison*

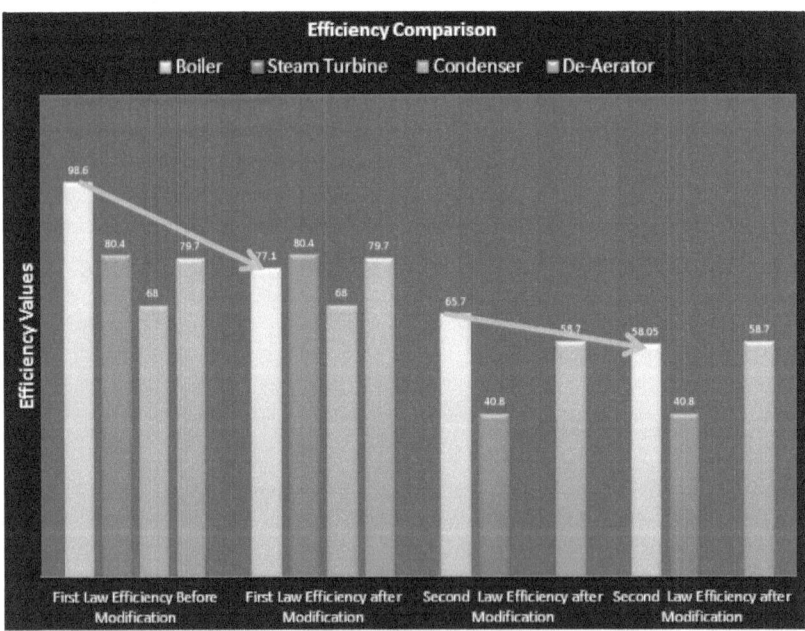

*Fig 4.22: Correlation Chart for Second
Law Efficiency Comparison*

The Second Law efficiency of boiler before modification is 35.52 % where as after modification is 31.37 %

*From the Efficiency Analysis comparison, it is found out that as availability increases, the second law efficiency decreases.*

### 4.15 Results and Discussions

The study yield following results

**Case 1:When LNG supply price is 14.5 USD per MMBTU**

1.1 System Availability before Modification, $A_s$ = 0.9085

1.2 System Reliability before Modification, $R_s$=0.002717

1.3.System Availability After Modification,$A_m$=0.9243

1.4.System Reliabilty After Modification $R_m$=0.003789

1.5. Percentage Improvement in System Availability =1.85%

1.6. Percentage Improvement in System Reliability =39.45%

1.7. Change in Process System Value = INR $2.7 \times 10^8$

1.8. Simple Pay back period= 2.98 years

1.9.Payback period incorporating reliability and availability=2.4 years

**Case 2:When LNG supply price is 24.75 USD per MMBTU**

2.1.System Availability before Modification, $A_s$ = 0.9085

2.2.System Reliability before Modification, $R_s$=0.002717

2.3.System Availability After Modification, $A_m$=0.9243

2.4.System Reliability After Modification $R_m$ =0.003789

2.5. Percentage Improvement in System Availability =1.85%

2.6 Percentage Improvement in System Reliability =39.45%

2.7 Change in Process System Value = - 9.1 x $10^7$ [Negative]

2.8 At supply price of LNG @24.75 USD per MMBTU, running the modified plant with LNG will yield loss. Hence the fuel to continue with furnace oil until the price issues are resolved.

3. First Law Efficiency of Boiler Before Modification = 98.6 %

4. First Law Efficiency of Steam Turbine Before Modification=80.4%

5. First Law Efficiency of Condenser Before Modification = 68%

6. First Law Efficiency of De-Aerator Before Modification =79.7%

7. First Law Efficiency of Boiler After Modification =77.1 %

9. First Law Efficiency of Steam Turbine After Modification=80.4%

10. First Law Efficiency of Condenser After Modification = 68%

11. First Law Efficiency of De-Aerator After Modification =79.7%

12.Second Law Efficiency of Boiler Before Modification = 65.7 %

13. Second Law Efficiency of Steam Turbine Before Modification=40.8 %

15. Second Law Efficiency of De-Aerator Before Modification =58.7 %

16. Second Law Efficiency of Boiler After Modification =58.05 %

17. Second Law Efficiency of Steam Turbine After Modification=80.4%

15. Second Law Efficiency of De-Aerator Before Modification =58.7 %

18. Net Station Energy Rejection Rate of Condenser before Modification = 2.25

19. Net Station Exergy Rejection Rate of Condenser before Modification = 0.25

18. Net Station Energy Rejection Rate of Condenser After Modification = 2.25

19. Net Station Exergy Rejection Rate of Condenser After Modification = 0.25

The system availability and reliability shows improved values after modification. The system availability and reliability values before modification are 0.9085 and 0.002717. The system availability and reliability after modification are 0.9243 and 0.003789. The percentage improvement in System availability is 1.85% where as Percentage improvement in System reliability is 39.45%. The higher percentage of system reliability shows the LNG conversion modification will optimize the system from a technical point of view. But commercially, due to socio political and economic conditions, the higher supply price of LNG as adversely affecting the modification implementation as running the plant art the current supply price will yield loss. The initial rate of 14.5 USD per MMBTU was a better price as it will give pay back in 2.4 years against a simple payback period of 2.98 years. It indicates that the modification will definitely result in improved system efficiency from an engineering point of view at an optimized rate of LNG price.

The first law efficiency of Steam Turbine is having a value 80.4% where as of Boiler is 98.6% before modification. The first law efficiencies after modification are 77.1% and 40.8 % respectively. The first law efficiencies of Steam Turbine, De-Aerator, and Condenser are same before and after modification. The reason being the thermodynamic parameters are not affected on account of modification.

The Second Law efficiency of Boiler before modification is 65.7% where as the efficiency after modification is 58.5 %. The efficiency is seen lower after modification and is based on RLNG feed rate 62.5 Kg/hr for one ton of steam. The feedback will be given to the facility owners and if could be lowered with out affecting the thermodynamic parameters, the second law efficiency could be further improved. However due to increase in Availability hours, the chance of increasing efficiency is less as it is seen that as availability increases, second law efficiency decreases. The second law efficiency is lower due to irreversibilities which are not accounted in first law and 40.8% is true value in case of efficiency of steam turbine.

The Second Law efficiency of the boiler is much lower than first law efficiency due to high degradation of energy which inreases the entropy.

In the condensers,energy-analysis results lead to the erroneous conclusion that almost all losses in electricity generation potential for are associated with the heat rejected by the condensers, while exergy analyses demonstrate quantitatively and directly that the condensers are responsible for little of these losses. This discrepancy arises because heat is rejected by the condensers at a temperature very near that of the environment. The characteristics of condensers can be seen more clearly by considering the 'net station condenser heat (energy) rejection rate' *R*energy, and the 'net station condenser exergy rejection rate' *R*exergy.

De –Aerator has a first law efficiency of 79.7% and a second law efficiency of 58.7%.

## 4.16 Recommendations

1. It is recommended to implement the process evaluation model in power plants to evaluate impact of modifications in terms of reliability, availability, payback period incorporating reliability and availability and impact of variations in LNG (fuel) prices.

2. It is necessary to install one more Forced Draft fan in addition to the existing one for redundancy as the system before and after modification has only one FD fan per boiler. If the FD fan fails it will lead to plant shut down.

3. The LNG price need to be stabilized at the rate or lower of 14.5 USD per MMBTU for the economic performance of the modified plant.

4. There are efficiency improvement oppurtunities in Boiler. The RLNG feed rate of 62.5 Kg/hr to be analysed to lower the value to further increase the second law efficiency of boiler.

# CHAPTER 5

# FUTURE WORK

1. Evaluation of Real Time Reliability Index of Captive Power Plant before and after modification.
2. Deriving the availability component in Second Law efficiency by establishing a mathematical relation that can be incorporated into efficiency calculation to substantiate the finding that "as availability increases second law efficiency decreases."

# CHAPTER 6

# CONCLUSIONS

1. The presented work study the modifications on the existing plant for the LNG conversion from furnace oil fired boiler.

2. The individual component/subsystem reliability and availability are calculated and also the system reliability and availability before and after modification are also evaluated.

3. The improved system reliability and availability indicate the modification will improve the performance of the modified plant.

4. The process evaluation model remains as an efficient tool in determining the process system value of the power plant

5. The process system value is positive in Case 1 where LNG supply price is 14.5 USD per MMBTU which demonstrate that the modification cost is recoverable.

6. However due to socio political and economic reasons the LNG supply price was increased to 24.75 USD per MMBTU.

7. The impact of increased price was evaluated using the process evaluation model and observed that the price is infeasile to run the plant.

8. Thus the impact of modifications in De super and flame burner system on the process system value of the 7MW captive power plant was assessed using the evaluation model and also impact of variation in fuel price is also assessed using the same model.

9. The first law and Second law efficiencies of main power plant components are evaluated before and after modification.

10. It is observed that as availability of Boiler increases Second Law Efficiency Decreases.

11. The erroneous conclusions based on higher values of efficiencies of main power plant components by first law is defended by Second Law Efficiency evaluation and actual efficiencies are found be low due to high degradation of energy and irreversibilities that are accounted in second law.

# REFERENCES

1. A. Rashad, and A. El Maihy, Energy and Exergy Analysis of a Steam Power Plant in Egypt, 13th International Conference on Aerospace Sciences and Aviation technology ASAT- *13,* May 26 – 28, 2009

2. AmirabedinEhsana, M. ZekiYilmazoglu -Design and Exergy Analysis of a Thermal Power Plant Using Different Types of Turkish Lignite, International Journal of Thermodynamics (IJoT) Vol. 14 (No. 3), pp. 125-133, 2011

3. Badino V, Baldo GL. LCA, instructions for use. Bologna: Progetto Leonardo Edition (in Italian); 1998.

4. Brian Wodka, Power-Plant Reliability, Availability, Maintainability, Military protocol being adapted for power plants,May 20, 2013,RMF Engineering Inc.; Baltimore, Md. | HPAC Engineering

5. Charles EE. Reliability and maintainability engineering. 1st ed. New Delhi: Tata McGraw-Hill Publishing Company Ltd; 2000.

6. Cornelissen RL, Marquart EN, Hirs GG. The value of the exergetic life cycle assessment besides the LCA. In: International proceedings of ECOS '99, Tokyo, Japan; 1999. p. 282–6.

7. D. Bradt,Use of reliability, availability and maintainability techniques to optimise system operation,Hydrocarbon Process, 76 (1997), pp. 63–65

8   Dennis J. Wilkins -Retired Hewlett-Packard Senior Reliability Specialist, currently a ReliaSoft Reliability Field Consultant,The Bathtub Curve and Product Failure BehaviorPart One - The Bathtub Curve, Infant Mortality and Burn-in,Issue 21, 2002

9   E. Carpaneto, G. Chicco, P. Mancarella, A. Russo,Cogeneration planning under uncertainty. Part I: Multiple time frame approach,Appl Energy, 88 (2011), pp. 1059–1067

10  E. Carpaneto, G. Chicco, P. Mancarella, A. Russo,Cogeneration planning under uncertainty. Part II: Decision theory-based assessment of planning alternatives,Appl Energy, 88 (2011), pp. 1075–1083

11  Egware H.Oand Obanor A.I, Energy Analysis of Omotosho Phase 1 Gas Thermal Power Plant,Department of Mechanical Engineering, University of Benin, P.M.B 1154, Benin City, Nigeria

12  Etienne Human, Tekniva Group, Sasolburg, South Africa,CarabTekniva Group – Asset Management & Reliability Engineering June 2012 No: C001

13  G. Ji, W. Wu, B. Zhang, H. Sun,A renewal-process-based component outage model considering the effects of aging and maintenance,Electr Power Energy Syst, 44 (2013), pp. 52–59

14  G.F.M. De Souza,Thermal power plant performance analysis,Elsevier Butterworth-Heinemann, London (2012)

15  Goel HD, Grievink J, Hetrder P, Weijnen MC. Integrating reliability optimization into chemical process. ReliabEngSyst Safe 2002;78:247–58.

16  H.PaulBarringer, Availability, Reliability, Maintainability, and Capability, P.E.Barringer& Associates, Inc. Humble, TX,Triplex Chapter Of The Vibrations Institute, Hilton Hotel Beaumont, Texas February 18, 1997

17  Hsieh YC, Chen TC, Bricker DL. Genetic algorithm for reliability design problems. MicroelectronReliab 1998;38:1599–605

| 18 | http://www.business-standard.com/article/economy-policy/captive-power-producers-turn-to-exchanges. |
| 19 | http://www.gasprocessingnews.com/features/201404/consider-factors-affecting-onshore-lng-plant-design.aspx |
| 20 | http://www.newindianexpress.com/cities/kochi/FACT-moves-to-LNG-from-Naphtha/2013/10/19/article1843215.ece# |
| 21 | J. Tang, Mechanical system reliability analysis using a combination of graph theory and Boolean function, ReliabEngSyst Safety, 72 (2001), pp. 21–30 |
| 22 | Jose K Jacob, Dr.P.V.Shouri, A deterministic reliability based model for process control,–International Journal of Production Technology and Management, Number 1, July-August (2010),pp 32-44 |
| 23 | K.B. Goode, J. Moore, B.J. Roylance, Plant machinery working life prediction method utilising reliability and condition monitoring data, ProcInstMechEng Part E: J Process MechEng, 214 (2000), pp. 109–122 |
| 24 | Kuo W, Prasad VR. An annotated overview of system-reliability optimization. IEEE Trans Reliab 2000;49(2):176–87. |
| 25 | L.R. James, D.B. David, U.R. Sabah, Engineering economics, Fourth Edition, Tata McGraw-Hill Companies, Inc., New York, 1996. |
| 26 | Lazzaretto A, Macor A, Mirandola A, Stoppato A. Potentialities and limits of exergoeconomics methods in the design, analysis and diagnosis of energy conversion plants. In: Proceedings of the international conference on advances in energy studies. Porto Venere, Italy; 1988. p. 515–30 |
| 27 | Lozano MA, Valero A. Theory of the exergetic cost. Energy 1993;18(9):939–60. |
| 28 | Tsatsaronis G, Winhold M. Exergoeconomic analysis and evaluation of energy conversion plants; part I: a new general methodology; part II: analysis of a coal-fired steam power plant. Energy 1985;10(1): 81–94. |

29 Lutz James, Lekov A, Chan P, Whitehead CD, Meyers S, McMahon J. Life-cycle cost analysis of energy efficiency design options for residential furnaces and boilers. Energy 2006;31:311–29.

30 M. Eti, S. Ogaji, S. Probert,Integrating reliability, availability, maintainability and supportability with risk analysis for improved operation of the AFAM thermal power-station,Appl Energy, 84 (2007), pp. 202–221

31 M. Ghazikhani, M. Ahmadzadehtalatapeh-Experimental investigation of exergy destruction in a 8-kW power plant, International Journal of Energy and Environment,*Volume 1, Issue 5, 2010 pp.815-822*

32 M. Mohan, O.P. Gandhi, V.P. Agrawal, Maintenance criticality index of a steam power plant: a graph theoretic approach,ProcInstMechEng Part A: J Power Energy, 218 (2004), pp. 619–636

33 M. Mohan, O.P. Gandhi, V.P. Agrawal, Systems modeling of a coal based steam power plant,ProcInstMechEng Part A: J Power Energy, 217 (2003), pp. 259–277

34 M. Mohan, O.P. Gandhi, V.P. Agrawal,Real-time efficiency index of a steam power plant: a systems approach,ProcInstMechEng Part A: J Power Energy, 220 (2006), pp. 103–131

35 M. Mohan, O.P. Gandhi, V.P. Agrawal,Real-time reliability index of a steam power plant: a systems approach,ProcInstMechEng Part A: J Power Energy, 222 (2008), pp. 355–369

36 M.F. Wani, O.P. Gandhi,Development of maintainability index for mechanical systems,ReliabEngSyst Safety, 65 (1999), pp. 259–270

37 M.N. Faisal, D.K. Banwet, R. Shankar,Quantification of risk mitigation environment of supply chains using graph theory and matrix methods,Euro J IndEng, 1 (1) (2007), pp. 22–39

38  M.R. Haghifam, M. Manbachi,Reliability and availability modelling of combined heat and power (CHP) systems,Electr Power Energy Syst, 33 (2011), pp. 385–393

39  N. Deo,Graph theory with applications to engineering and computer science,Prentice Hall, New Delhi (2007)

40  N. Dev, Samsher, S.S. Kachhwaha, R. Attri,GTA-based framework for evaluating the role of design parameters in cogeneration cycle power plant efficiency,Ain Shams Eng J, 4 (2) (2013), pp. 273–284

41  N. Dev, Samsher, S.S. Kachhwaha,Systemmodeling and analysis of a combined cycle power plant,Int J SystAssurEng Manage (2012) doi: http://dx.doi.org/10.1007/s13198-012-0112-y

42  O.P. Gandhi, V.P. Agrawal, K.S. Shishodia,Reliability analysis and evaluation of systems,ReliabEngSyst Safety, 32 (1991), pp. 283–305

43  Odum HT. Environmental accounting, emergy and decision making. New York: Wiley; 1995.

44  P.V. Shouri, P.S. Sreejith, Algorithm for break even availability allocation in process system modification using deterministic valuation model incorporating reliability, Energy Conversion and Management 49 (2008) 1380-1387

45  P.V. Shouri, P.S. Sreejith, Need for incorporating reliability and availability in payback calculations,Industrial Management and Organisation,Volume 31,Issue 2,December 2008

46  Patrick DTO. Practical reliability engineering. 4th ed. England: John Wiley & Sons Ltd; 2002.

47  R.H. Kehlhofer, J. Warner, H. Nielsen, R. Bachmann,Combined cycle gas and steam turbine power plants,PennWell, Tulsa (1999)

48  R.K. Garg, V.P. Agrawal, V.K. Gupta,Selection of power plants by evaluation and comparison using graph theoretical methodology,Electr Power Energy Syst, 28 (2006), pp. 429–435

49 Raviprakashkurkiya andSharadchaudhary,Energy Analysis of Thermal Power Plant,International Journal of Scientific & Engineering Research Volume 3, Issue 7, July-2012 1 ISSN 2229-5518

50 S. Carlier, M. Coindoz, L. Deneuville, L. Garbellini, A. Altavilla, Evaluation of reliability, availability, maintainability and safety requirements for manned space vehicles with extended on-orbit stay time,ActaAstronautica, 38 (2) (1996), pp. 115–123

51 S. Kulkarni,Graph theory and matrix approach for performance evaluation of TQM in Indian industries,TQM Mag, 17 (6) (2005), pp. 509–526

52 S.C. Kaushik, V.SivaReddy, S.K.Tyagi - Energy and exergy analyses of thermal power plants:A review,Renewable and Sustainable Energy Reviews 15 (2011) 1857–1872

53 Sarang J. Gulhane1, Prof. Amit Kumar Thakur, A. P. Pathre, Scope of Improving Energy Utilization in Coal Based Co-Generation on Thermal Power Plant -Review, International Journal of Modern Engineering Research (IJMER) www.ijmer.com Vol. 3, Issue. 5, Sep - Oct. 2013 pp-2615-2625

54 Sciubba E. Exergy as a direct measure of environmental impact. In: Proceedings of international mechanical engineering conference and exposition – ASME Winter Annual Meeting Nashville, USA; 1999. p. 231–8.

55 Srinath LS. Reliability engineering. 3rd ed. New Delhi: Affiliated East West Press; 1991.

56 Szargut J. Depletion of unrestorable natural exergy resources as a measure of the ecological cost. In: International proceedings of ECOS '99, Tokyo, Japan. p. 42–5.

57 T. Raj, R. Attri,Quantifying barriers to implementing Total Quality Management (TQM) Euro J IndEng, 4 (3) (2010), pp. 308–335

58  V Ranganathan, Damodar Mall Captive Power Generation: What are the Economics ?Vol. *12, No. 2, April-June 1987*

59  Valero A. Thermoeconomics as a conceptual basis for energyecological analysis. In: Proceedings of the international conference on advances in energy studies. Porto Venere, Italy; 1988. p. 415– 44.

60  Von Spakovsky MR, Frangopoulos CA. A global environomic approach for energy systems analysis and optimization; part I and part II. In: Proceedings of the international conference on energy systems and ecology, ASME, vol. 1. Cracow, Poland; 1993. p. 123–44.

61  Vundela Siva Reddy, Subhash Chandra Kaushik, Sudhir Kumar Tyagi,-An Approach to Analyse Energy and Exergy Analysis of Thermal Power Plants: A Review, NarayaLalPanwar, *Smart Grid and Renewable Energy*, 2010, 1, 143-152

62  W. Tabakoff,Compressor erosion and performance deteriorationA1AA/ASME 4th joint fluid mechanics, plasma dynamics, and lasers conference, vol. 37ASME Publication FED, Atlanta (GA) (1986)

63  Zaita, G. Buley, G. Karlsons,Performance deterioration modeling in aircraft gas turbine engines.JEng Gas Turb Power, 120 (1998), pp. 344–349

64  http://www.reliasoft.in/BlockSim/maintainability_analysis.htm

# NOMENCLATURE

## SYMBOLS

| | |
|---|---|
| ΔH | Difference in Enthalpy |
| A | Availability |
| $A_A$ | Achieved Availability |
| $A_{BEP}$ | Break even availability of modified process system |
| $A_I$ | Inherent Availability |
| $A_i$ | Steady State Availability |
| $A_m$ | Availability after modification |
| $A_O$ | Operational Availability |
| $A_s$ | Process System Availability |
| b | Pay back period |
| C | Bulk velocity of working fluid |
| C | Cost of process system components and equipments |
| $C_m$ | Cost of Modification |
| E | expected yearly savings due to modification |
| $E_I$ | Energy at Inlet |
| $E_O$ | Energy at Outlet |

| | |
|---|---|
| g | Acceleration due to gravity |
| g | expected percentage growth of operating / maintenance cost per year |
| H | Hours of Operation |
| He | Helium |
| hr | hour |
| i | rate of interest |

## SYMBOLS

| | |
|---|---|
| K | Kelvin |
| k Cal | kilo Calories |
| kg | kilo gram |
| m | mass |
| mm | milli metres |
| n | Expected life of Process System in Years |
| $N_2$ | Nitrogen |
| O | Operating Cost of first Year |
| °C | Degree Celsius |
| $O_m$ | Operational Cost after modification |
| $O_s$ | Operational Cost at Steady State |
| P/A | Present Value Given Annual Rate |
| $Q_k$ | Heat transfer to system from source |
| R | Hourly production rate |
| R(t) | Reliability expressed as a function of time |
| $R_{energy}$ | Net Station Energy Rejection rate |
| $R_{exergy}$ | Net Station Exergy Rejection rate |
| $R_{S(t)}$ | System Reliability for a given time period "t" |

| | |
|---|---|
| T | Temperature of Source |
| U | Unit cost of production |
| V | Process System Value |

## NOMENCLATURE

## SYMBOLS

| | |
|---|---|
| $V_c$ | Change in Process System Value |
| W | Net work developed by the system |
| $W_T$ | Turbine Work |
| Z | Altitude of stream above sea level |
| $\eta_I$ | First Law Efficiency |
| $\eta_{II}$ | Second Law Efficiency |
| $\lambda$ | constant repair rate |
| $\mu$ | constant mean repair rate |
| $\Psi$ | Exergy |

## SUBSCRIPTS

| | |
|---|---|
| A | Achieved |
| BEP | Break even Period |
| c | change |
| I | Inherent |
| i | Steady state |
| m | modification |
| m | modification |
| O | operational |
| o | out |
| s | System/steady state |
| T | Turbine |

# ABBREVIATIONS

| APH | Air Pre Heater |
|-----|----------------|
| ASME | American Society of Mechanical Engineers |
| BTU | British Thermal Unit |
| CBM | Condition Based Maintenance |
| CExLCA | Cumulative Exergy Costing Accounting |
| CHP | Combined Heat and Power |
| CPP | Captive Power Plant |
| CPU | Central Processing Unit |
| CWHE | Coil Wound Heat Exchanger |
| DMR | Dual Mixed Refrigerant |
| DSH | De Super Heater |
| EEA | Extended Exergy Accounting |
| ETA | Event Tree Analysis |
| ExLCA | Exergetic Life Cycle Assessmenr |
| FACT | Fertilizers and Chemicals Travancore |
| FBA | Fish Bone Analysis |
| FD | Forced Draft |
| FMEA | Failure Mode Effect Analysis |
| FMECA | Failure Mode Effect and Criticality Analysis |
| FO | Furnace Oil |
| FSH | Final Super Heater |

# ABBREVIATIONS

| FTA | Fault Tree Analysis |
|-----|---------------------|
| HILP | High Impact Low Probability |
| ID | Induced Draft |

| INR | Indian Rupees |
|---|---|
| LCA | Life Cycle Assessment |
| LCC | Life Cycle Costing |
| LNG | Liquified Natural Gas |
| LPG | Liquified Petroleum Gas |
| LTSH | Low Temperature Super Heater |
| MAMT | Mean Active Maintenance Time |
| MCR | Maximum Continuous Rating |
| MDT | Mean Down Time |
| MMBTU | Million Metric British Thermal Unit |
| MMTpy | Million Tons per Year |
| MR | Mixed Refrigerant |
| MTBF | Mean Time Between Failures |
| MTBM | Mean Time Between Corrective and Preventive Maintenance |
| MTTR | Mean Time to Repair |
| MW | Mega Watts |
| PdM | Predictive based Maintenance |
| PFA | Predictive Failure Analysis |
| PM | Preventive Maintenance |

## NOMENCLATURE

## ABBREVIATIONS

| PSH | Platen Super Heater |
|---|---|
| RAM | Reliability, Availability and Maintainability |
| RAMS | Reliability, Availability, Maintainability, Safety |
| RCA | Root Cause Analysis |
| RCFA | Root Cause Failure Analysis |

| | |
|---|---|
| RCM | Reliability Centred Maintenance |
| RLNG | Re-Gasified Liquified Natural Gas |
| RM | Reactive Maintenance |
| RT | Real Time |
| RTEI | Real Time Efficiency Index |
| RTRI | Real Time Reliability Index |
| SCAPH | Steam Coiled Air Pre Heater |
| SCF | Standard Cubic Feet |
| SCM | Standard Cubic Metre |
| SH | Super Heater |
| SPP | Steam Power Plant |
| TPH | Tonne per Hour |
| USD | United States Dollars |
| VLSI | Very Large Scale Integrated Circuits |
| VPF | Variable Permanent System Structure Function |

# INDEX